Modi's India

Modi's India

Vision, Transformation & the Road Ahead

Amit Prakash Sharma

Copyright Notice

Publisher Information:

Published by Amazon Kindle Direct Publishing, 2024

ISBN: 9798877648234

Imprint: Independently Published

Permissions Email: amitprakashsharma@outlook.com

Author Website: https://amitprakashsharma.com/

Disclaimer

The information presented in this book is intended for general informational purposes only and should not be seen as professional advice. The views and opinions expressed herein are solely those of the author and may not necessarily align with the official policies or positions of any agencies, organizations, employers, companies, or individuals. This book represents the culmination of extensive research and analysis, reflecting the author's interpretations of the events, policies, and personalities discussed.

While every effort has been made to ensure the accuracy and reliability of the information at the time of publication, the dynamic and evolving nature of political and social affairs means that circumstances and facts may change over time. Therefore, the author and publisher cannot guarantee the complete accuracy, reliability, suitability, or availability of this work's information, products, services, or related graphics for any particular purpose. Readers are cautioned that any reliance on the material in this book is strictly at their own risk.

Declaration

This book is an independent publication and has not been authorized, sponsored, or otherwise approved by any government bodies, political parties, or individuals mentioned herein. The content is not designed to promote or demote any political views or ideologies. Instead, it represents Amit Prakash Sharma's personal views and analyses based on information obtained from public sources. The interpretations and conclusions drawn in this book are the author's own and should be considered as one of many perspectives on the events or policies described. Readers are encouraged to approach the content with an open mind and consider it part of a broader dialogue on the subject matter.

Amit Prakash Sharma

DEDICATION

This book is dedicated to the serene embrace of dawn as the sun's first rays tenderly kiss India's vibrant lands.

To the soul of India - its people.

From the snow-dusted peaks of the Himalayas to the sun-soaked beaches of the south, from the farmers tilling the earth with unwavering resolve to the bright minds shaping the future with their innovations, this dedication is a homage to the indomitable spirit of the nation.

It is to the dreams woven into the fabric of everyday life, the resilience that courses through its citizens' veins, and the unity that thrives amidst the wondrous diversity.

This book is for you, the people of India, who embody the essence of transformation and resilience, mirroring the vision of a leader who aspires to harness this spirit for the nation's ascendance on the global stage.

TABLE OF CONTENTS

Dedication i

Epigraph... v

Preface vii

Acknowledgements ix

Introduction: The Modi Epoch Unveiled xi

Part I: The Genesis Of Modi's Vision 1

   Chapter 1: Humble Beginnings to Prime Minister........... 3

   Chapter 2: Gujarat's Helmsman 15

   Chapter 3: Crafting a Campaign of Hope 27

Part II: Transformative Policies and Governance 41

   Chapter 4: Economic Reformation............................. 43

   Chapter 5: Digital India and Beyond 61

   Chapter 6: Revolutionizing Health and Education 69

   Chapter 7: Environmental Paradigm Shift.................... 81

   Chapter 8: A New Era of Defense and Diplomacy 89

Part III: Cultural and Societal Evolution....................... 101

   Chapter 9: Navigating the Social Mosaic 103

   Chapter 10: Redefining National Identity..................... 115

   Chapter 11: The Media Landscape............................. 127

Part IV: Challenges and Critiques 141

   Chapter 12: The Contours of Criticism 143

   Chapter 13: Democracy and Secularism Debated 157

Part V: Projecting the Future 167

Chapter 14: India's Place on the World Stage.................169

Chapter 15: Legacy in the Making 183

Conclusion: The Road Ahead for Modi's India................201

Epilogue: Reflective Thoughts on India's Potential Directions.........209

About the Author 217

Call to Action: Engaging with India's Future 219

EPIGRAPH

"In the great tapestry of time,
every thread is essential;
every weave tells a story of change, resilience, and progress.

Let us be the weavers of change,
the harbingers of progress,
and the guardians of resilience."

\- Narendra Modi

PREFACE

As I narrate the transformative era of Modi's India, I am reminded of a crisp autumn morning in Varanasi, the spiritual heartland of India, where the ancient and the contemporary converge in a harmonious symphony. It was there, amidst the echoing chants and the serene flow of the Ganges, that the inspiration for this book took root. This narrative is not just an exploration of policies or a chronicle of events; it is a voyage into the heart of a nation once ancient and vibrantly young, guided by a leader whose vision for India is as boundless as the sky.

Prime Minister Narendra Modi's tenure has been a significant socio-political and economic transformation for India. From the corridors of power in New Delhi to the smallest villages, his policies have aimed at inclusivity, technological advancement, and global integration, redefining India's stature on the world stage. However, the journey has been as challenging as it has been rewarding, marked by bold decisions that have sparked both admiration and controversy.

This book aims to offer readers a window into the complexities of governing the world's largest democracy, where every decision affects the lives of over a billion people. Through a blend of personal reflections, in-depth analysis, and conversations with those whom Modi's policies have directly impacted, I aspire to present a nuanced portrait of an India navigating the delicate balance between tradition and modernity, economic growth, and environmental sustainability.

As you turn these pages, I invite you to join me in exploring the intricate mosaic of Modi's India - a land of diversity, dreams, and dynamism. Whether you seek to understand the geopolitical shifts under his leadership, the digital revolution that has permeated Indian society, or the grassroots movements shaping the rural landscape, this book promises a journey through the many layers that make up contemporary India.

In writing this preface, I hope to set the stage for a narrative that is as enlightening as it is engaging, offering insights into not just the what and the how but also the why of Modi's vision and initiatives. It is a story of a nation in flux, resilient and hopeful people, and a leader with a grand vision for a New India.

ACKNOWLEDGMENTS

In making this book a journey as enriching as it has been enlightening, I have been fortunate to cross paths with many individuals whose support, wisdom, and encouragement have been the wind beneath my wings. This section is a humble token of gratitude towards each of them, for their collective contributions have shaped this narrative into what it is today.

Firstly, my heartfelt thanks to the myriad of voices from across India whose stories and perspectives have brought depth and authenticity to this narrative. From the farmers in the lush fields of Punjab to the tech entrepreneurs of Bangalore, your experiences have been the cornerstone of this exploration.

I am eternally grateful to my academic mentors and peers, whose rigorous discussions and invaluable insights helped sharpen my understanding of India's socio-political landscape. Your guidance has been a beacon of light in navigating the complex interplay of factors that define Modi's India.

Thanks to the research assistants and interns who toiled alongside me, sifting through data, reports, and archives, ensuring that every fact mentioned within these pages stands the test of scrutiny and lends credibility to our discourse.

I would be remiss if I did not acknowledge the unwavering support of my family, whose patience and love provided me with the space and peace to pursue this endeavor. To my spouse, for the endless cups of tea and the listening ear, and to my children, for their understanding and cheer, you are my rock.

Lastly, to the readers who embark on this journey through the pages of this book, your engagement and curiosity ultimately give meaning to this work.

It is my earnest hope that this book sparks thoughtful conversations, offers new perspectives, and perhaps, in its small way, contributes to a broader understanding of the remarkable journey that is Modi's India.

In weaving together this tapestry of acknowledgments, I am reminded of the interconnectedness of our efforts and the shared spirit of inquiry that drives us forward. Here's to the collective endeavor of understanding and shaping the narrative of a nation that continues to inspire and challenge us in equal measure.

INTRODUCTION

THE MODI EPOCH UNVEILED

"In the journey of every nation, there are moments that bring the opportunity not just for incremental change, but for historic transformation. India is living that moment now."

— Narendra Modi

Opening Remarks

In the annals of India's storied political history, the ascension of Narendra Modi to the Prime Minister's office in May 2014 heralded a new era. Marked by fervent hopes and formidable challenges, Modi's premiership promised to steer India towards uncharted territories of development and global recognition. This period, widely recognized as "The Modi Epoch," has been a testament to the power of visionary leadership and its capacity to redefine the contours of a nation's destiny.

Contextualizing Modi's Leadership

Before Narendra Modi's tenure, India stood at a critical juncture, grappling with economic slowdowns, governance inefficiencies, and a palpable sense of disillusionment among its populace.

The quest for transformative leadership was in the air as citizens across the demographic spectrum yearned for a paradigm shift that could rejuvenate the nation's socio-political and economic fabric.

Modi's Premise

Narendra Modi emerged as a figure of significant political intrigue against this backdrop, promising an era of unprecedented growth and governance. With a track record of proactive governance as the Chief Minister of Gujarat, Modi positioned himself as the harbinger of a "New India" – a nation thriving on economic prosperity, digital innovation, and robust global standing.

Vision for a New India

Modi's vision for India was articulated through ambitious promises that aimed to transcend traditional development paradigms. Initiatives targeting economic overhaul, digital transformation, and governance reforms were set against the objective of enhancing India's stature on the global stage.

The reception of Modi's vision was a blend of optimism and skepticism, reflecting the diverse aspirations and apprehensions of the Indian electorate.

The Modi Epoch

The Modi Epoch is characterized by its bold policy initiatives and a distinct shift in governance models. This period marks a significant departure from conventional politicking, with a pronounced emphasis on policy-driven governance.

The thematic depth of Modi's tenure, encompassing economic reform, the digital revolution, cultural nationalism, and strategic international engagements, outlines the broad spectrum of changes underway.

Character and Leadership

Modi's leadership style is a study in contrasts – deeply rooted in traditional Indian values yet remarkably adept at leveraging modern technology and governance practices. His journey from the Chief Minister of Gujarat to the Prime Minister of India is a narrative of relentless pursuit, visionary leadership, and strategic acumen.

This evolution reflects a multifaceted leader poised to navigate India through its complexities and challenges.

Structure of the Book

This book is structured to provide a comprehensive exploration of Narendra Modi's transformative impact on India. Each part and chapter is designed to delve into distinct aspects of his tenure, from economic policies and digital initiatives to cultural shifts and international diplomacy.

While celebrating India's strides under Modi, the book also engages critically with the controversies and challenges that have marked his leadership.

Goals for the Reader

The aim is for readers to gain a nuanced understanding of Narendra Modi's legacy, extending beyond simplistic narratives to appreciate the profound changes shaping India.

It encourages an active engagement with the narrative, inviting readers to partake in the dialogue about India's future trajectory.

Why This Book? Why Now?

In a time when information is abundant yet clarity is scarce, "Modi's India" stands as a clarion call for insight and understanding.

Crafted for those who yearn to discern the truth behind the tumult, this book offers a meticulous analysis that connects the past with the present, shedding light on the future.

Part I: The Genesis of Modi's Vision delves into the roots of Modi's ambition, presenting a narrative that intertwines personal history with a political vision.

Part II: Transformative Policies and Governance critically examines the hallmark reforms and initiatives of Modi's tenure. From economic innovation to digital advancements, healthcare transformations, and environmental strategies, this section scrutinizes the essence of Modi's governance.

Part III: Cultural and Societal Evolution navigates the profound changes within India's societal fabric under Modi's leadership, offering an insightful exploration of cultural nationalism and the evolving media landscape.

Part IV: Challenges and Critiques presents a balanced examination of the controversies and debates that have encircled Modi's administration, fostering a space for reflective discussion on the intricacies of governance.

Part V: Projecting the Future speculates on the enduring impact of Modi's policies, contemplating the future trajectory of India's development and its implications for global dynamics.

Conclusion

The introduction of "The Modi Epoch Unveiled" sets the stage for a journey through one of the most pivotal periods in contemporary Indian history. By connecting Modi's past achievements with future possibilities, the book invites readers to explore the depths of Modi's impact on India.

This exploration is not just about understanding a political tenure but about comprehending the transformative journey of a nation poised on the brink of global ascendancy.

Your Invitation to Explore

"Modi's India: Vision, Transformation, & the Road Ahead" is an intellectual journey designed to engage, enlighten, and provoke thought. Whether you are an ardent supporter, a critical observer, or simply curious about the global narrative, this book unfolds a compelling panorama of Modi's India, inviting you to engage in a dialogue that transcends geographical and ideological boundaries.

This book is your gateway to the complexities, triumphs, and challenges of Narendra Modi's India. As you turn each page, you will unravel the multifaceted narrative of a nation at a historical juncture, poised to redefine its role in the world order under Modi's stewardship. Embark on this exploration with "Modi's India" and discover the untold stories behind the vision, transformation, and pathway forward. Your perception of India—and perhaps of leadership and transformative change—will be forever altered.

This introduction primes readers for a deep dive into the complexities, achievements, and challenges of Narendra Modi's India, offering a balanced perspective that fosters a comprehensive understanding of his enduring impact on the nation's trajectory.

PART I:
THE GENESIS OF MODI'S VISION

"My vision for India is rapid transformation, not gradual evolution."
— Narendra Modi

CHAPTER 1

HUMBLE BEGINNINGS TO PRIME MINISTER

"Hard work never brings fatigue. It brings satisfaction."

— Narendra Modi

This chapter embarks on Narendra Modi's remarkable journey from his early years in a small town in Gujarat to his rise as the Prime Minister of India. It explores the foundational experiences that shaped his vision for India and his steadfast commitment to service and leadership.

Introduction

In the small town of Vadnagar, nestled within the heart of Gujarat, a young boy's journey commenced—a journey that would transcend the confines of his humble beginnings and navigate the complex labyrinth of Indian politics, ultimately leading him to the highest echelon of power as the Prime Minister of India. This is the story of Narendra Modi, a tale of resilience, ambition, and transformative leadership.

Born into a family where scarcity was the norm, Modi's early life was far from the corridors of power and privilege.

Instead, it was rooted in the rich cultural heritage of Gujarat amidst the struggles of everyday life that shape the indomitable spirit of those who dare to dream beyond their immediate circumstances. It was here, in the narrow lanes of Vadnagar, that Modi's perspectives on life, society, and governance were molded. These formative years were not just about overcoming challenges but about imbibing a vision that would one day aspire to transform a nation.

The significance of Modi's early years extends beyond mere biographical interest. They serve as a testament to the power of determination, the importance of vision, and the relentless pursuit of excellence. Through his journey, Modi embodies the aspirations of millions, representing a beacon of hope for those who seek to rise above their conditions and contribute to the broader narrative of nation-building.

This chapter seeks to unravel the layers of Narendra Modi's early experiences—his family background, his education, and his ideological formation. By delving into these aspects, we aim to provide a foundational understanding of the factors that have shaped his character and political ambitions. It is a narrative that navigates through his initial political journey, setting the stage for his eventual leadership of India, a leadership that seeks to marry vision with action, tradition with modernity, and governance with grassroots empowerment.

As we embark on this journey, let us explore the humble beginnings of Narendra Modi, understanding how a boy from Vadnagar became the Prime Minister of India and, more importantly, what this transformation signifies for the future of India.

Early Life and Education

Narendra Damodardas Modi was born on September 17, 1950, in the small town of Vadnagar, in the Mehsana district of Gujarat, India.

The third of six children to Damodardas Mulchand Modi and Hiraben Modi, Narendra's childhood was steeped in the modesty of a lower-middle-class family. His father ran a small tea stall at the Vadnagar railway station, where Narendra would often lend a hand, serving tea to travelers. This early exposure to the struggles of life did not dampen his spirit; instead, it instilled in him a resilience and work ethic that would define his later years.

The socio-economic backdrop of Modi's upbringing played a crucial role in shaping his worldview. Vadnagar, with its historical significance and cultural richness, provided a nurturing ground for Modi's early interest in broader societal issues. Despite the financial constraints, Modi's parents were determined to provide their children with an education, a decision that laid the groundwork for Narendra's future.

Modi was an average student but displayed a keen interest in debating and theatre, which were instrumental in honing his public speaking skills. His educational journey was marked by a determination to learn and evolve, characteristics that remained with him throughout his life. Modi completed his higher secondary education in Vadnagar itself. Despite the hardships, the importance of education was deeply ingrained in him by his family and community.

It was during these formative years that Modi developed an interest in the Rashtriya Swayamsevak Sangh (RSS), a Hindu nationalist volunteer organization. The RSS's emphasis on discipline, nationalism, and selfless service resonated with Modi, drawing him closer to its fold. His interaction with RSS members and participation in the local shakhas (branches) provided him with an ideological grounding that would later influence his political philosophy. The early exposure to the RSS's activities not only shaped Modi's ideological beliefs but also his understanding of leadership and governance. It was here that he learned the importance of grassroots organization, a principle that he would carry forward into his political career.

Modi's journey through his early life and education is a testament to the impact of one's environment and experiences in shaping future leaders.

It underscores the notion that leadership qualities are often forged in the crucible of early struggles and challenges. As Modi moved from his childhood into his teenage years, his involvement with the RSS became more pronounced, marking the beginning of his journey into the realm of political activism and public service. This phase of his life was characterized by a deepening commitment to the values he had been introduced to in his early years, setting the stage for his eventual entry into formal politics.

Involvement with the RSS

Narendra Modi's initiation into the Rashtriya Swayamsevak Sangh (RSS) during his formative years was a pivotal moment in his life. It was within the folds of the RSS that Modi found a channel for his nationalist fervor and a platform to engage actively in social and political activities. His early involvement with the RSS, a right-wing Hindu nationalist volunteer organization, played a crucial role in shaping his ideological outlook and his approach to leadership and governance.

Ideological Grounding and Values:

The RSS's ideology, centered on fostering national pride, cultural unity, and social reform, deeply influenced Modi. The organization's emphasis on discipline, dedication, and a hierarchy-based structure appealed to Modi's inherent qualities of hard work and determination. Through his participation in the daily meetings (shakhas), Modi imbibed the RSS's ethos of selfless service to the nation, which later became a cornerstone of his political and governance philosophy.

Leadership Qualities and Work Ethic:

Modi's engagement with the RSS provided him with numerous opportunities to develop and demonstrate his leadership abilities.

He was involved in organizing local and regional events, which honed his organizational and management skills. Modi's dedication and capability quickly earned him recognition within the organization, leading to his involvement in more significant projects and responsibilities. His time with the RSS also instilled in him a robust work ethic and the ability to mobilize and motivate people toward a common goal, traits that would define his political career.

Political Ideology:

The RSS's influence on Modi's political ideology cannot be overstated. It laid the foundation for his belief in strong governance, nationalism, and the importance of cultural identity. Modi's early experiences with the RSS also shaped his views on social and economic issues, driving him to pursue policies that aimed at inclusivity and development during his political career. His commitment to the principle of "Antyodaya" (uplifting the most underprivileged) is a reflection of the RSS's impact on his approach to governance.

Transition to Active Politics:

Modi's deepening involvement with the RSS eventually facilitated his transition into active politics. Recognized for his dedication and leadership skills, he was recommended by the RSS to the Bharatiya Janata Party (BJP), a political party with close ideological ties to the RSS. This transition marked the beginning of a new chapter in Modi's life, where he would apply the principles and skills learned during his time with the RSS to navigate the complexities of Indian politics.

Modi's journey from a young volunteer in the RSS to a key figure in the BJP exemplifies how his early experiences and ideological grounding provided the blueprint for his political career. It highlights the significant role that the RSS played in shaping not only Modi's values and beliefs but also his approach to leadership and governance.

Entry into Politics

Narendra Modi's transition from an RSS Pracharak (campaigner) to a key player in the Bharatiya Janata Party (BJP) in the early 1980s was a turning point in his life. This move was not merely a change of roles but a strategic shift that placed Modi at the forefront of Indian politics, allowing him to leverage his skills and ideological foundation in a broader arena.

Initial Roles and Responsibilities:

Upon joining the BJP, Modi was assigned roles that capitalized on his organizational skills and understanding of grassroots movements. His initial responsibilities included overseeing the party's activities in various regions, coordinating with party workers, and organizing rallies and events. Modi's ability to mobilize support and manage large-scale events was quickly recognized, leading to his rapid ascent within the party hierarchy.

Political Strategies and Acumen:

Modi's early years in the BJP were marked by his innovative approach to political strategies. He was instrumental in strengthening the party's presence in Gujarat, employing a mix of traditional outreach and modern campaigning techniques. His efforts were pivotal in the BJP's electoral successes in the state, contributing to its emergence as a significant political force. Modi's knack for understanding public sentiment and leveraging it to the party's advantage was evident during this period, showcasing his political acumen and strategic thinking.

Leadership Style Development:

The BJP provided Modi with a platform to develop and exhibit his leadership style further. Characterized by decisiveness, a focus on efficiency, and a strong vision for development, Modi's approach to leadership was both admired and criticized.

However, it was his ability to connect with the masses and articulate a clear vision for the future that set him apart from his contemporaries.

Rise within the Party Ranks:

Modi's contributions to the party's growth and his effective leadership did not go unnoticed. His roles became increasingly significant, culminating in his appointment as the General Secretary of the BJP, a position that allowed him to influence the party's direction at the national level. Modi's tenure as General Secretary saw him playing a crucial role in the party's national campaigns and strategy formulations.

Preparation for State Leadership:

The culmination of Modi's political journey within the BJP was his selection as the party's candidate for the Chief Minister of Gujarat in 2001. This decision was influenced by Modi's proven track record, leadership qualities, and vision for the state's development. His appointment as Chief Minister marked the beginning of a new era in Gujarat's politics and set the stage for Modi's emergence as a national leader. Modi's entry into politics and subsequent rise within the BJP highlights the interplay between his ideological foundation, leadership abilities, and political acumen. It was this combination that propelled him from the grassroots of the RSS to the helm of Gujarat's governance, preparing him for the national stage and, ultimately, the Prime Minister's office.

Leadership in Gujarat

Narendra Modi's tenure as the Chief Minister of Gujarat, beginning in 2001, was marked by a series of transformative initiatives aimed at economic development, infrastructure enhancement, and governance reforms. Under his leadership, Gujarat embarked on a journey of rapid growth, often referred to as the "Gujarat Model" of development.

Ascent to Chief Minister:

Modi's ascent to the Chief Minister's office was a turning point in Gujarat's political landscape. Taking charge in the aftermath of an earthquake in 2001 that had devastated parts of the state, Modi's initial challenge was to lead the reconstruction efforts. His administration's effective response to the disaster set the tone for his governance style, characterized by a focus on efficiency, innovation, and direct communication with the public.

Economic Growth and Development:

One of the hallmarks of Modi's tenure in Gujarat was the emphasis on economic growth and industrial development. Through policies aimed at attracting investment, improving infrastructure, and simplifying regulatory processes, Gujarat saw a significant increase in its industrial output. The state became an attractive destination for both domestic and international investors, contributing to its reputation as an economic powerhouse.

Agricultural Reforms and Water Management:

Modi introduced several initiatives to improve agriculture in Gujarat, a sector critical to the state's economy. The "Krishi Mahotsav" (Agriculture Festival) and the "Sujalam Sufalam" canal network project were aimed at increasing agricultural productivity and water conservation. These efforts led to substantial improvements in crop yields and water management, benefiting thousands of farmers across the state.

Controversies and Criticisms:

Modi's tenure as Chief Minister was not without controversy, the most significant being the 2002 Gujarat riots. The communal violence that engulfed the state led to widespread criticism of Modi's administration, with allegations of inadequate response and even complicity.

While Modi has been cleared of wrongdoing by the Supreme Court of India, the riots remain a contentious part of his legacy.

Governance and Public Policy:

Beyond economic development, Modi's governance model in Gujarat was noted for its emphasis on technology and innovation in public administration. Initiatives like the "Jyotigram Yojana" for rural electrification and the use of e-governance tools improved service delivery and government transparency. These policies not only enhanced the quality of life for many Gujaratis but also showcased Modi's vision of a modern, efficient, and inclusive administration.

Preparation for National Leadership:

Modi's achievements in Gujarat, coupled with his dynamic leadership style, set the stage for his emergence as a national leader. The "Gujarat Model" of development became a key part of his political narrative, demonstrating his capability to lead transformative change on a larger scale. As Modi's popularity grew, so did the calls for his leadership at the national level, eventually leading to his nomination as the BJP's prime ministerial candidate in the 2014 general elections.

Modi's leadership in Gujarat was a critical period that defined his political identity and showcased his governance philosophy. It was during this time that he established himself as a decisive leader capable of implementing broad-scale reforms, setting the foundation for his future role as Prime Minister of India.

Election Victory and Early Days as Prime Minister

The 2014 general elections in India were a watershed moment, not only for Narendra Modi but for the entire nation.

This election saw Modi transitioning from a state leader to the national stage, bringing with him a vision of transformative change and development that resonated with millions across the country.

Innovative Campaign Strategies:

Modi's election campaign was notable for its extensive use of digital media and technology, a first in India's electoral history. Leveraging social media platforms, mobile messaging, and digital rallies, Modi was able to connect with a diverse and widespread electorate, transcending geographical and demographic barriers. This digital outreach was complemented by a relentless schedule of public rallies across the country, where Modi's oratory skills and direct communication style captivated the masses.

The campaign also focused on a narrative of hope and change, promising good governance, economic revitalization, and a strong stance on national security. Modi's image as a decisive and visionary leader, contrasted with the incumbent government's perceived indecisiveness and corruption, played a significant role in shaping public opinion.

The 2014 General Elections:

The result of the 2014 elections was historic, with the Bharatiya Janata Party (BJP) securing an absolute majority in the Lok Sabha, India's lower house of Parliament, for the first time in its history. This victory marked a significant shift in Indian politics, with Modi at the helm of the world's largest democracy.

Initial Actions as Prime Minister:

Upon taking office, Modi embarked on a series of initiatives aimed at fulfilling his campaign promises. One of his first actions was the launch of the 'Make in India' campaign, designed to turn India into a global manufacturing hub.

This was followed by a slew of reforms and initiatives such as the 'Swachh Bharat Abhiyan' (Clean India Mission) to improve sanitation and cleanliness and the 'Jan Dhan Yojana' to increase access to banking services for the unbanked population.

Modi's early days in office were also marked by a proactive approach to foreign policy, with efforts to strengthen ties with neighboring countries as well as major world powers. His emphasis on diplomacy and international relations was aimed at positioning India as a key player on the global stage.

Conclusion

Narendra Modi's journey from a small-town boy in Vadnagar to the Prime Minister of India is a narrative of determination, vision, and transformative leadership. His early life, steeped in the challenges and experiences of ordinary Indians, shaped his political ideology and governance style, emphasizing development, inclusivity, and effective administration.

As Modi embarked on leading India, his vision for the country was clear: to catalyze a transformation that would elevate India's stature on the world stage while ensuring the prosperity and well-being of its citizens.

The early days of his premiership set the tone for what was to come, marking the beginning of an era that promised to redefine India's trajectory towards growth and development.

This chapter not only charts Modi's ascent to the highest office in India but also sets the stage for exploring the policies, governance, and societal changes that his leadership would bring, as detailed in the subsequent chapters of "Modi's India: Vision, Transformation, & the Road Ahead."

The narrative journey from Narendra Modi's humble beginnings to his role as Prime Minister encapsulates a transformative vision for India, bridging past achievements with future aspirations and setting a comprehensive foundation for understanding the profound impact of his leadership on the nation's path forward.

CHAPTER 2

GUJARAT'S HELMSMAN

"What Gujarat has achieved is through hard work.
Not by mere speeches. Work on the ground is the only way forward."

— Narendra Modi

Analyzing Modi's tenure as Chief Minister of Gujarat, this chapter focuses on key policies and their outcomes, showcasing how his leadership in Gujarat served as a blueprint for his vision for India.

Introduction

In the early 2000s, Gujarat stood at a crossroads of potential and challenge, harboring aspirations to transcend its traditional agricultural economy and leapfrog into industrialization and modernity. Into this setting stepped Narendra Modi, a figure whose ascent to the Chief Minister's office in 2001 marked the beginning of a transformative era for the state. This chapter delves into Modi's tenure as Gujarat's helmsman, exploring the governance style, policies, and controversies that defined this period and offering insights into the leadership qualities that would later shape his prime ministerial vision for India.

15

Introduction to Gujarat's Leadership

Before Modi's tenure, Gujarat was known for its entrepreneurial spirit, but it faced significant hurdles in infrastructure, power supply, and water management. The state was ripe for a leadership that could harness its potential and address these challenges head-on. Modi's ascent to power was met with a blend of optimism and skepticism. On the one hand, his reputation as a dynamic leader from within the Bharatiya Janata Party (BJP) promised decisive governance; on the other, his lack of administrative experience at the state level raised questions about his ability to navigate the complexities of Gujarat's development needs.

Ascending to Power

Narendra Modi's appointment as Chief Minister was a pivotal moment in Gujarat's political landscape. It came amidst internal party dynamics and a need for fresh leadership to rejuvenate the BJP's image and governance in the state. Modi's rise was characterized by his portrayal as a leader focused on development and governance, setting a tone of pragmatism and progress. His initial priorities were clear: to revitalize Gujarat's economy, ensure a stable power supply, and lay the groundwork for infrastructural development.

Governance and Policy Initiatives

Under Modi's leadership, Gujarat embarked on an ambitious journey of economic and infrastructural development. The state's economic policies were geared towards attracting investment, promoting industrialization, and fostering a business-friendly environment. The Gujarat model of development, characterized by its emphasis on growth, governance, and development, became a subject of national and international attention.

Economic Development:

Modi's government implemented policies that significantly boosted industrial growth, with special emphasis on sectors like petrochemicals, agriculture, and services.

The promotion of Special Economic Zones (SEZs) and the Vibrant Gujarat summits played crucial roles in positioning the state as an investment destination.

Infrastructure and Urban Development:

Infrastructure projects, including the development of road networks, power plants, and urban centers, were prioritized. Efforts to ensure 24/7 electricity through the Jyotigram Yojana transformed the rural and urban landscapes of Gujarat, enabling economic activities to flourish.

Agriculture and Water Management:

Initiatives such as the Sardar Sarovar Dam and the Krishi Mahotsav emphasized water conservation, irrigation, and modern agricultural practices, leading to notable improvements in agricultural productivity.

Social Policies:

Modi's administration also focused on education and healthcare reforms. The introduction of various programs aimed at improving quality and access marked steps towards addressing social development gaps.

Leadership Style

Modi's leadership and governance style were marked by an emphasis on efficiency, innovation, and technology. His hands-on approach and decision-making capability were evident in the rapid implementation of projects and reforms. However, this approach also sparked debates on centralized control, with critics arguing that it led to an over-concentration of power.

Controversies and Critiques

Modi's tenure was not without controversy. The 2002 Gujarat riots were a significant blot on his leadership, eliciting national and international condemnation.

The environmental impact of rapid industrialization and the sustainability of Gujarat's economic growth model were also points of criticism. However, Modi's administration consistently defended its policies, emphasizing the overall development and progress of the state.

Achievements and Recognition

Despite the controversies, Gujarat under Modi received numerous accolades for its development model. The state's growth story and governance model were recognized both nationally and internationally, setting the stage for Modi's emergence as a prime ministerial candidate.

Conclusion: From State to National Vision

Modi's tenure as Chief Minister was a period of significant transformation for Gujarat, shaping his political and leadership identity. The Gujarat model became a cornerstone of his vision for India, reflecting his aspirations for governance, development, and economic growth at the national level. As we transition to the next chapter, the narrative shifts from state-level leadership to Modi's aspirations and challenges on the national stage, foreshadowing his journey from the Chief Minister of Gujarat to the Prime Minister of India.

Economic Development

Under Narendra Modi's stewardship, Gujarat's economic landscape underwent significant transformation. Central to this was the Gujarat model of development, which emphasized rapid industrial growth, infrastructure development, and an investor-friendly environment.

Modi's government streamlined business processes, reducing bureaucratic hurdles and promoting ease of doing business, which attracted both domestic and international investors.

Key Economic Policies:

Promotion of Industrialization: Modi's tenure saw an aggressive push for industrialization, with policies designed to attract investment in key sectors such as manufacturing, petrochemicals, and pharmaceuticals. The establishment of Special Economic Zones (SEZs) played a pivotal role in this regard, offering incentives for companies to set up operations in Gujarat.

Vibrant Gujarat Summit: Initiated in 2003, these biennial summits became a hallmark of Modi's economic agenda, successfully showcasing Gujarat as a global business hub and facilitating investment commitments from across the world.

Impact on State's Growth:

Gujarat recorded impressive growth rates during Modi's tenure, with the state's GDP growth often outpacing the national average. This period saw substantial increases in per capita income and a reduction in unemployment rates, highlighting the success of Modi's economic policies.

Infrastructure and Urban Development

Modi's governance model also placed a strong emphasis on infrastructure development as a cornerstone for economic growth. Recognizing the importance of robust infrastructure, his administration undertook several ambitious projects aimed at improving connectivity, power supply, and urban living standards.

Major Projects:

Power Sector Reforms: The Jyotigram Yojana, aimed at providing uninterrupted power supply to rural areas, was a game-changer for the state's economy. This initiative not only facilitated rural development but also ensured a stable power supply to the industrial sector.

Road and Urban Development: Significant investments were made in road infrastructure, improving connectivity within the state and with neighboring regions. Urban development projects focused on modernizing cities, making them more livable and business-friendly.

Transformation of Gujarat's Landscape:

The impact of these initiatives was profound, with Gujarat achieving notable improvements in its physical and economic infrastructure. The state emerged as a model for effective infrastructure development, contributing to its overall growth and development narrative.

Conclusion

The detailed exploration of economic development and infrastructure projects under Narendra Modi's leadership in Gujarat highlights the strategic approach taken to transform the state's economy and physical landscape. These initiatives were instrumental in positioning Gujarat as a development model, reflecting Modi's governance style characterized by efficiency, innovation, and a focus on results.

Leadership Style and Economic Achievements

Efficiency and Decision-Making:

Modi's governance was marked by a focus on efficiency and quick decision-making processes. This was evident in the rapid implementation of projects and reforms, which often bypassed the bureaucratic delays typical in other parts of India.

His administration was known for setting clear targets and timelines for project completion, which was crucial for the timely execution of infrastructure and development projects.

Innovation and Technology:

A hallmark of Modi's tenure in Gujarat was the embrace of innovation and technology to enhance governance. Initiatives like the e-Governance projects under the Gujarat model streamlined government processes and improved service delivery to citizens. This not only boosted the state's efficiency but also reduced corruption and increased transparency.

Centralized Control vs. Collaborative Governance:

While Modi's hands-on leadership and centralized decision-making style were credited for Gujarat's swift development, they also sparked debates about the concentration of power and the marginalization of dissenting voices. Critics argued that this approach led to a governance model that, while effective in driving economic growth, sometimes overlooked broader social and environmental concerns.

Broader Impact on Modi's Political Career

National Recognition:

The success of Gujarat's development model under Modi's leadership significantly boosted his national profile. The tangible achievements in economic growth, infrastructure development, and governance efficiency provided a solid foundation for his image as a development-oriented leader, setting the stage for his rise to the prime ministership.

Leadership Persona:

Modi's leadership style in Gujarat—characterized by assertiveness, a focus on development, and a strong public relations strategy—became integral to his political persona.

This image played a key role in his campaign for the national leadership, appealing to voters across India who sought decisive and efficient governance.

Critiques and Controversies:

However, the same leadership style that propelled Gujarat's development also attracted criticism, particularly regarding the handling of the 2002 riots and environmental management issues. These controversies followed Modi into the national arena, where they continue to evoke debate and discussion.

Conclusion

Narendra Modi's leadership style, marked by efficiency, innovation, and a strong focus on development, was instrumental in transforming Gujarat's economic and infrastructural landscape. While his tenure as Chief Minister was characterized by significant achievements, it also raised questions about centralized governance and its social and environmental ramifications. As Modi transitioned to national leadership, these aspects of his governance approach continued to influence perceptions and expectations, underscoring the complexity of his political legacy.

Environmental Challenges

Rapid Industrialization:

While Gujarat's economic policies successfully attracted investment and boosted industrial growth, they also led to environmental concerns. The rapid expansion of industries, particularly in sectors like petrochemicals, raised issues related to pollution, resource depletion, and environmental degradation.

Water Management:

Although initiatives like the Sardar Sarovar Dam and the Krishi Mahotsav improved irrigation and agricultural productivity, they also sparked debates over water resource management, displacement of communities, and ecological impacts.

Balancing water needs for agriculture, industry, and human consumption presented significant governance challenges.

Case Studies:

Industrial Pollution: Regions like Vapi, Ankleshwar, and the Golden Corridor faced severe industrial pollution challenges, affecting air, water, and soil quality.

Sardar Sarovar Dam: While it's a monumental project for water resource management and power generation, it also led to displacement issues and environmental concerns.

Social Challenges

Inclusive Development: The critique often leveled against the Gujarat model was its focus on growth at the expense of inclusiveness. Questions were raised about the extent to which the benefits of economic growth reached marginalized communities, including the rural poor, minorities, and other vulnerable groups.

Labor and Employment: While industrial growth created job opportunities, there were also concerns about the nature of employment, labor rights, and working conditions in the newly established industries and SEZs.

Broader Impact on Modi's Governance

Navigating Critiques:

These environmental and social challenges required nuanced governance strategies to navigate. The critiques provided learning opportunities for Modi's administration to address sustainability and inclusiveness more effectively, aspects that would become increasingly important in his national leadership role.

Policy Adjustments:

In response to these challenges, there were efforts to introduce policy adjustments aimed at environmental conservation and social welfare. Initiatives to promote renewable energy and enhance social welfare programs can be seen as responses to the critiques of the Gujarat model.

Conclusion

The environmental and social challenges encountered during Modi's tenure as Chief Minister of Gujarat highlight the complexities of governance in the face of rapid development. These challenges not only shaped policy adjustments within the state but also informed Modi's approach to governance at the national level, emphasizing the need for a balanced approach that considers economic growth alongside environmental sustainability and social inclusiveness.

Achievements and Legacy

Economic Growth and Industrialization:

Modi's tenure in Gujarat is marked by significant economic growth and industrialization, positioning the state as an investment hub in India. The Gujarat model of development, characterized by its focus on infrastructure, efficiency, and business-friendly policies, garnered national and international attention.

Infrastructure Development:

The strides made in infrastructure—ranging from power supply and road connectivity to urban development—transformed Gujarat's physical and economic landscape, facilitating industrial growth and improving living standards.

Innovation in Governance:

Modi's use of technology and innovation in governance, exemplified by initiatives like the Jyotigram Yojana and e-governance projects, set new standards for administrative efficiency and service delivery.

Critiques and Challenges

Environmental and Social Sustainability:

The rapid pace of industrialization under Modi's leadership raised concerns about environmental degradation and the sustainability of natural resources. Additionally, questions about the inclusiveness of economic growth highlighted the challenges of ensuring benefits reached all sections of society.

Handling of Controversies:

The 2002 Gujarat riots remain a significant and controversial aspect of Modi's tenure as Chief Minister. The handling of the riots and their aftermath has been a subject of intense debate and scrutiny, affecting perceptions of Modi's leadership.

Implications for National Leadership

Governance Model:

The Gujarat model, with its emphasis on development, governance, and economic growth, became a cornerstone of Modi's vision for India.

This model shapes his policies and initiatives at the national level, aiming to replicate Gujarat's success on a larger scale.

Balancing Development with Sustainability:

The environmental and social challenges encountered in Gujarat underscore the importance of balancing economic development with environmental sustainability and social equity.

These challenges inform Modi's approach to national policies, particularly in sectors like renewable energy, welfare schemes, and social development initiatives.

Leadership Style:

Modi's centralized decision-making and hands-on leadership style, while effective in driving development in Gujarat, also spark ongoing discussions about governance approaches at the national level. The balance between decisive leadership and democratic inclusiveness remains a key aspect of his tenure as Prime Minister.

Conclusion

Narendra Modi's tenure as Chief Minister of Gujarat laid the groundwork for his ascent to national leadership, showcasing his governance style, policy priorities, and the challenges he faced.

The legacy of his tenure in Gujarat, with its blend of achievements and critiques, provides valuable insights into the complexities of governance and the nuances of leading the world's largest democracy.

As Modi continues to navigate India's path on the national and international stages, the lessons learned from Gujarat remain integral to understanding his vision and strategies for the country's future.

The exploration of Narendra Modi's tenure in Gujarat reveals a multifaceted legacy that shapes his role as Prime Minister.
As we move forward, the impact of his governance style, policy initiatives, and leadership decisions continues to influence India's development trajectory and its place on the global stage.

CHAPTER 3

CRAFTING A CAMPAIGN OF HOPE

"A campaign built on the foundation of hope and inclusive development has the power to transcend the barriers of caste, creed, and politics, uniting a nation in its pursuit of progress.
We walk together, we move together, we think together, we resolve together, and together we take this country forward."

— Narendra Modi

The narrative of Modi's ascent to the Prime Minister's office, underscored by his vision for a new India, is detailed. The chapter explores the strategies and messages that resonated with millions of Indians, propelling Modi to a historic win.

Introduction: Setting the Stage

The chapter begins in the bustling, diverse landscape of India shortly before the 2014 general elections. It was a time marked by widespread discontent with the incumbent government, plagued by corruption scandals and perceived inefficiency. The Indian populace, a vibrant amalgamation of cultures, languages, and religions, was clamoring for change.

Amidst this backdrop of societal yearning for a new direction, the stage was set for a political transformation that would reshape the nation's future.

The Prelude to Campaign

The narrative unfolds in the early 2010s, detailing the political and social climate that laid the groundwork for a significant electoral shift. India, despite its economic strides, faced numerous challenges: rural distress, urban-rural disparities, and a young population desperate for employment opportunities. The public's frustration with the status quo was palpable, and there was a collective aspiration for a leader who could usher in an era of prosperity and stability.

This section delves into the specifics of the pre-election scenario, capturing the mood of a nation on the brink of change. It paints a picture of the socio-political landscape, highlighting key incidents and public sentiments that signaled a desire for a fresh leadership paradigm.

Modi's Nomination: The Prelude to Ascension

The journey to Narendra Modi's nomination as the Bharatiya Janata Party's (BJP) prime ministerial candidate was neither straightforward nor devoid of controversy.

This section explores the intricate political maneuvers, internal party dynamics, and the broader public and media reactions leading up to his nomination.

Background to Modi's Rise within the BJP

Modi's ascent within the BJP ranks was marked by his tenure as the Chief Minister of Gujarat, a position he held from 2001 to 2014. His leadership in Gujarat was characterized by a focus on development, industrialization, and governance reforms.

These achievements, coupled with his charismatic leadership and oratorical skills, solidified his reputation as a results-driven administrator. However, Modi's candidacy was not without its detractors, both within and outside the BJP.

His tenure in Gujarat was marred by the 2002 riots, a deeply divisive event that sparked significant controversy and debate about his leadership during the crisis. This section discusses the balancing act between Modi's proven administrative track record and the lingering shadows of past controversies.

Circumstances and Controversies around His Nomination

The decision to nominate Modi was the culmination of a series of strategic discussions within the BJP, influenced by a groundswell of support from the party's rank and file, as well as its ideological mentor, the Rashtriya Swayamsevak Sangh (RSS). The narrative explores the internal party dynamics, the role of senior party leaders, and the strategic considerations that led to Modi's emergence as the prime ministerial candidate.

This part of the chapter also addresses the broader political context in India at the time, including the role of media, public opinion, and the reaction from rival political parties. It highlights the polarized views on Modi's nomination, reflecting the broader national debate on governance, leadership, and the direction in which India was headed.

Through detailed analysis and rich detailing, this section sets the stage for understanding how Narendra Modi's nomination as the BJP's prime ministerial candidate was a pivotal moment in India's political landscape, setting the tone for a campaign that promised hope and change.

The Vision for a New India: Articulating Hope and Change

Narendra Modi's campaign for the Prime Minister's office was anchored in a compelling vision for a New India. This vision was articulated through a narrative that promised development, good governance, and national pride—resonating deeply with a populace eager for change.

This section delves into the specifics of Modi's vision and the strategic communication that made it compelling to diverse sections of Indian society.

Articulating the Vision

Modi's vision for India was multifaceted, focusing on accelerating economic growth, enhancing India's global standing, and improving the quality of governance. He promised to build a nation where every citizen could achieve their potential, free from the shackles of corruption and bureaucratic inertia.

This part of the chapter examines the key aspects of Modi's vision for development, including the emphasis on digital infrastructure, manufacturing, and the creation of a more inclusive society. The narrative details how this vision was communicated to the public, leveraging Modi's skills as an orator and the strategic use of media. It explores the themes of hope and revitalization that underpinned Modi's message, drawing parallels to global political campaigns that have harnessed similar sentiments to mobilize support.

Themes of Hope and Change

This section explores the thematic elements that were central to Modi's campaign, particularly the emphasis on hope and the promise of change. It draws comparisons with other global leaders and campaigns, such as Barack Obama's "Hope" campaign, to contextualize Modi's strategy within a broader trend of political messaging focused on positive change.

The analysis highlights how Modi's campaign successfully tapped into the collective aspirations of the Indian populace, offering a narrative of hope and progress that was both inspiring and aspirational. It discusses how these themes were woven into the campaign's messaging, rallies, and public engagements, creating a wave of support for Modi's vision.

Communication Strategies to Resonate with Diverse Societal Sections

Modi's campaign masterfully tailored its message to resonate with different segments of Indian society, from rural voters seeking economic upliftment to urban professionals desiring efficient governance. This section examines the multifaceted communication strategies employed by the campaign, including the innovative use of digital media, targeted messaging, and Modi's direct engagement with the electorate through rallies and public addresses.

It underscores the campaign's emphasis on inclusivity and national unity, highlighting how Modi's vision was presented as a blueprint for an India that could bridge the gap between its rich diversity and common aspirations. This chapter segment not only provides a comprehensive understanding of the vision that propelled Narendra Modi to the Prime Minister's office but also offers insights into the sophisticated campaign strategies that turned this vision into a resonant message for millions of Indians.

Innovative Use of Digital Media in the Campaign

The 2014 general elections marked a watershed moment in Indian electoral politics, largely due to Narendra Modi's pioneering use of digital media as a campaign tool. This section delves into the strategic deployment of social media platforms, digital outreach initiatives, and the creation of a digital-first campaign that revolutionized political communication in India.

Revolutionizing Voter Engagement through Digital Platforms

Modi's campaign team recognized early on the potential of digital media to reach and engage India's burgeoning internet user base, particularly the youth.

This part of the chapter explores the various digital channels used by the campaign, including social media platforms like Twitter, Facebook, and YouTube, to disseminate Modi's vision for India and mobilize support.

The analysis includes a look at specific campaigns, such as the "Chai pe Charcha" (Discussion over Tea) initiative, which used digital platforms to facilitate direct interaction between Modi and voters across the country. It highlights how these digital engagements allowed the campaign to bypass traditional media gatekeepers, delivering Modi's message directly to the electorate.

The Role of Data and Analytics in Shaping Campaign Strategies

A significant aspect of Modi's digital campaign was the sophisticated use of data analytics to tailor messages and target voters effectively. This section examines how the campaign leveraged big data to understand voter preferences, monitor social media sentiment, and optimize outreach efforts.

It discusses the integration of analytics with on-ground campaign strategies, illustrating how data-driven insights informed the planning of rallies, the focus of speeches, and the allocation of resources across key battleground states.

Impact of Digital Media on Voter Perception and Engagement

The innovative use of digital media not only expanded the campaign's reach but also played a crucial role in shaping voter perception of Modi as a forward-thinking leader attuned to the needs of a new generation of Indians. This part of the chapter assesses the impact of digital campaigning on voter engagement, highlighting how it contributed to building a groundswell of support for Modi.

The narrative draws on examples of viral social media campaigns, interactive online events, and the use of mobile technology to illustrate the transformative effect of digital media on political communication.

It also addresses the challenges and criticisms faced by the campaign in its digital outreach efforts, providing a balanced view of its successes and limitations. This section of the chapter underscores the strategic foresight of Modi's campaign in harnessing digital media, setting a new benchmark for political campaigning in India and offering valuable lessons for future electoral strategies worldwide.

Building Modi's Personal Brand

The transformation of Narendra Modi from a regional leader to a national prime ministerial candidate was underpinned by a meticulously crafted personal brand that resonated with the electorate's desire for decisive and transformative leadership.

This section explores the multifaceted approach to building Modi's public image, focusing on the narratives, communication strategies, and the portrayal of his personal journey that collectively contributed to his brand as a leader capable of ushering in a new era for India.

Crafting the Image of a Decisive Leader

Modi's personal brand was carefully constructed to emphasize his image as a decisive and effective administrator capable of delivering significant change. This part of the chapter examines the various elements of Modi's public persona, including his reputation for strong governance in Gujarat, his focus on development and economic growth, and his commitment to eradicating corruption.

The narrative also delves into how Modi's communication strategy highlighted his decision-making capabilities and problem-solving approach, setting him apart from the political establishment and aligning with the electorate's yearning for efficient governance.

The Narrative of Personal Journey

A compelling aspect of Modi's brand was the narrative of his personal journey from humble beginnings to becoming the Prime Ministerial candidate. This section outlines Modi's early life, his rise through the ranks of the BJP and the RSS, and the challenges he overcame along the way.

The story of Modi's ascent, characterized by hard work, dedication, and resilience, was leveraged to reinforce his connection with the common man and to illustrate his understanding of the challenges faced by ordinary Indians.

It discusses how this narrative was communicated to the public through speeches, social media, and campaign materials, contributing to Modi's appeal as a self-made leader.

Contrasting with the Political Establishment

Modi's branding strategy also involved positioning him as an outsider to the traditional political establishment, capable of bringing fresh perspectives and approaches to governance.

This part of the chapter contrasts Modi's image with that of his competitors, highlighting how his promise of change and development was made more compelling by the perceived inefficiencies and corruption associated with the incumbent government.

The analysis covers the strategic use of media and public appearances to underscore Modi's distinctiveness from the political status quo, enhancing his appeal to voters disillusioned with conventional politics.

This section of the chapter provides a comprehensive overview of how Narendra Modi's personal brand was developed and deployed to create a powerful narrative that played a crucial role in his ascent to the Prime Minister's office. It underscores the significance of personal branding in political campaigns and the impact of effectively communicated leadership qualities on electoral success.

Election Campaign Challenges

The path to Narendra Modi's historic victory in the 2014 general elections was fraught with numerous challenges. These ranged from addressing criticisms and controversies linked to his past, navigating the complex landscape of Indian politics to articulating and defending his policy proposals amidst intense scrutiny.

This section delves into the major hurdles faced by Modi's campaign and the strategies employed to overcome them, highlighting the resilience and adaptability of his campaign team.

Addressing Criticisms and Controversies

Central to the challenges faced by Modi was the need to address and navigate the criticisms related to his tenure as the Chief Minister of Gujarat, especially the 2002 riots.

This part of the chapter examines how Modi's campaign approached these controversies, focusing on the messaging strategies used to counteract negative perceptions and highlight Modi's governance record.

The narrative explores the fine balance struck by the campaign in acknowledging past events while steering the conversation towards Modi's vision for the future of India. It discusses the role of media engagements, public addresses, and digital platforms in crafting a counter-narrative that emphasizes development and inclusive growth.

Debates and Policy Questions

The campaign also had to contend with vigorous debates around economic policies, development models, and social issues. This section analyzes the discourse surrounding Modi's policy proposals, including the criticisms from opposition parties and the scrutiny from the media and public. It outlines how the campaign articulated Modi's economic agenda, focusing on job creation, infrastructure development, and improving the business environment.

The chapter details the strategic use of data, expert endorsements, and case studies from Gujarat to bolster Modi's credentials as a leader capable of delivering economic prosperity.

Navigating the Political Landscape

Another significant challenge was navigating the intricate political landscape of India, with its diverse electorate, regional variations, and the complexities of coalition politics. This part of the chapter describes the strategic alliances formed by the BJP, the role of regional leaders in the campaign, and the efforts to appeal to a broad spectrum of voters.

It highlights the campaign's adaptability in addressing regional issues, customizing messages to local contexts, and engaging with different communities to build a comprehensive support base.

This section provides an insightful look into the multifaceted challenges faced by Narendra Modi's campaign and the innovative strategies that enabled it to surmount these hurdles. It offers a nuanced understanding of the complexities involved in electoral politics and the critical importance of strategic communication and adaptability in achieving political success.

The 2014 General Election: Strategy and Outcome

The culmination of Narendra Modi's campaign efforts and strategic planning was vividly demonstrated in the 2014 general elections. This pivotal moment in Indian political history not only showcased the effectiveness of Modi's campaign strategies but also marked a significant shift in the nation's political landscape.

This section provides an in-depth analysis of the election strategy, the execution of the campaign in its final weeks, and the sweeping victory that brought Modi to power.

Election Strategy and Execution

In the lead-up to the elections, Modi's campaign team implemented a multi-pronged strategy that capitalized on digital media, extensive public rallies, and targeted messaging to key demographic and geographic segments. This part of the chapter delves into the strategic decisions that defined the campaign's final push, including the focus on battleground states, the mobilization of grassroots support, and the innovative use of technology to engage voters and monitor campaign performance.

The narrative highlights how the BJP's organizational strength, combined with the RSS's volunteer network, played a crucial role in executing a highly coordinated campaign. Special attention is given to the data-driven approach that informed the targeting of campaign resources, ensuring maximum impact in swing constituencies.

The Election Outcome

The results of the 2014 general elections were nothing short of historic, with the BJP securing an absolute majority in the Lok Sabha, a feat not achieved by any party since 1984.

This section details the election outcomes, focusing on the significant gains made by the BJP across diverse regions of India and the factors contributing to the party's sweeping victory.

It examines the public and political reactions to the election results, capturing the mood of the nation as it embarked on a new chapter with Modi at the helm. The analysis includes reflections on the role of Modi's personal appeal, the effective use of campaign strategies, and the desire for change among the Indian electorate as key drivers of the BJP's unprecedented success.

Reflecting on the Campaign's Success

The chapter concludes this section by reflecting on the strategic elements that underpinned the success of Modi's campaign. It considers the implications of the election results for Indian democracy, the BJP's position within the political landscape, and the expectations placed on Modi's government.

This comprehensive account of the 2014 general election strategy and outcome offers valuable insights into the dynamics of electoral politics in India, the power of effective campaign management, and the decisive impact of leadership in shaping political fortunes.

Conclusion: Reflecting on the Mandate for Change

The historic victory of Narendra Modi in the 2014 general elections was more than just a political triumph; it was a resounding mandate for change from the people of India.

This concluding section reflects on the significance of the election outcome, the expectations placed upon Modi and the BJP, and the forward-looking perspective that characterizes the anticipation of Modi's governance and policies.

The Mandate for Change

The sweeping victory achieved by Modi and the BJP was a clear signal from the electorate for a decisive shift in governance, economic policy, and national development. This part of the chapter explores the public's aspirations for Modi's tenure as Prime Minister, focusing on the desire for effective governance, transparency, and rapid economic growth.

The narrative delves into the broader implications of the election results, considering how the mandate reflected a collective yearning for a government that could deliver on the promise of a New India. It discusses the expectations set for Modi to implement his vision of development, good governance, and enhanced global standing for India.

Anticipation of Governance

With the mandate firmly in hand, the anticipation of Modi's governance style and the implementation of his policies became topics of national and international interest.

This section outlines the initial steps taken by Modi's government to address the high expectations, including efforts to streamline government operations, initiatives to boost economic growth, and policies aimed at improving the lives of ordinary Indians.

The chapter highlights the challenges and opportunities that lay ahead for Modi's administration, considering the complexities of implementing wide-ranging reforms in a diverse and populous country like India.

It provides a forward-looking perspective on the potential for transformative policies and governance styles that could redefine India's trajectory in the years to come.

Setting the Stage for the Future

In concluding, the chapter positions the 2014 general elections as a pivotal moment in India's democratic journey, setting the stage for a period of potential transformation under Modi's leadership. It reflects on the role of leadership, vision, and strategic campaigning in achieving political success while also acknowledging the weight of the responsibilities that come with a mandate for change.

The conclusion serves as both a reflection on a significant electoral victory and an anticipation of the governance and policies that would characterize Modi's tenure as Prime Minister. It offers readers a comprehensive understanding of the political, social, and technological dynamics that contributed to one of the most significant electoral victories in India's recent history, setting the groundwork for an in-depth exploration of Modi's impact on India's future.

With the conclusion of "Crafting a Campaign of Hope," we've provided a detailed account of Narendra Modi's strategic ascent to the Prime Minister's office, highlighting the vision, strategies, and narrative that defined this critical period. This chapter not only offers insights into the complexities of electoral politics but also sets the stage for examining the transformative impact of Modi's policies and governance style in the subsequent chapters.

PART II:
TRANSFORMATIVE POLICIES AND GOVERNANCE

"The government's job is good governance for everybody.
My government will make policies for the welfare of the masses,
not for a select few."
— Narendra Modi

CHAPTER 4

ECONOMIC REFORMATION

"Our economic reforms are not just policy changes but a commitment to empowering every Indian, ensuring that growth benefits everyone."

— Narendra Modi

This chapter critically examines Narendra Modi's economic policies, including demonetization and the implementation of the Goods and Services Tax (GST). It delves into their intentions, the challenges they faced, and their impact on transforming India's economic landscape.

Introduction

India was at a critical juncture in the years leading up to 2014. The nation grappled with several economic challenges—rampant inflation, widespread corruption, and bureaucratic inefficiencies that stifled growth and innovation. Against this backdrop, Narendra Modi stepped into the role of Prime Minister with promises of economic rejuvenation. His vision was clear: transforming the Indian economy through bold and unprecedented reforms to foster growth, ensure transparency, and enhance efficiency.

Modi's economic agenda was ambitious and controversial, featuring a mix of demonetization, the introduction of the Goods and Services Tax (GST), and several initiatives to boost the Indian economy's global standing. Each of these policies was designed not just as an economic measure but as a transformative shift towards a new India—an India that would not only compete on the global stage but also offer an inclusive and sustainable development model.

The path to economic reformation under Modi's leadership was far from smooth. It was a journey marked by bold decisions that often sparked intense debate within India and internationally. This chapter delves into the core of Modi's economic policies, examining their intentions, implementations, and the myriad impacts they have had on the fabric of the Indian economy.

Economic Context

Before Narendra Modi's tenure, the Indian economy was beset with significant challenges. Inflation rates were high, eroding the average citizen's purchasing power and complicating the business environment. Corruption was endemic, permeating various levels of governance and public service, leading to a lack of faith in the system and hindering foreign investment. Bureaucratic inefficiencies further exacerbated these issues, with red tape and a lack of clear policy directions slowing down economic progress and innovation.

Against this backdrop, Modi's vision for economic reform was not just seen as a policy shift but as a necessary overhaul of the existing system. He promised to address these foundational issues head-on, aiming to revitalize the economy and set India on a rapid growth and development path.

Demonetization: Announcement and Implementation

One of the most defining moments of Modi's economic policy was the announcement of demonetization on November 8, 2016. In a dramatic and unexpected television address to the nation, Modi declared that the ₹500 and ₹1,000 banknotes—the highest denominations in circulation and accounting for over 86% of the currency in use—would be invalid overnight. The government's objectives were manifold: to curb black money, combat corruption, fight terrorism financing, and promote digital transactions.

The immediate aftermath of demonetization was chaotic. Citizens thronged banks and ATMs in a desperate scramble to exchange or deposit their now-defunct notes, leading to widespread panic and confusion. The short-term impacts were palpable—small businesses suffered due to a sudden contraction in cash liquidity, and the rural economy, heavily dependent on cash transactions, faced unprecedented challenges. However, the narrative of demonetization is not one-sided. The long-term outcomes painted a more complex picture.

There was a significant increase in digital payment adoption across the country, a surge in tax compliance, and a push towards the formalization of the economy. Yet, critiques of demonetization also abound, questioning its effectiveness in achieving its stated goals and pointing to the economic disruption it caused.

Goods and Services Tax (GST): Concept and Rollout

Another cornerstone of Modi's economic reforms was the implementation of the Goods and Services Tax (GST) in July 2017. Hailed as the most significant tax reform since India's independence, GST aimed to unify the country's complex tax structure into a comprehensive tax system, thereby increasing tax compliance and simplifying the tax regime for businesses.

The rollout of GST marked a significant shift in how businesses operated across state lines, promoting a more unified national market. However, the transition was not without its challenges. Small and medium enterprises (SMEs), in particular, struggled to navigate the new tax system, facing difficulties with compliance and the increased administrative burden. The government responded with several adjustments and amendments to the GST framework, easing the transition and addressing the business community's concerns.

Economic Growth and Job Creation

Under Modi's leadership, the Indian economy witnessed periods of robust growth. Key indicators such as GDP growth and foreign direct investment (FDI) showed positive trends, reflecting the broader impact of his economic policies. However, the issue of employment remained contentious. While the government pointed to initiatives like "Make in India" and "Skill India" as drivers of job creation, critics argued that the pace of job creation was not keeping up with the number of entrants into the job market, leading to debates over "jobless growth."

Banking and Financial Sector Reforms

Banking sector reforms were another critical area of focus. Efforts to address non-performing assets (NPAs) and the recapitalization of public sector banks were undertaken to bolster the banking sector's health. Financial inclusion initiatives, most notably the Pradhan Mantri Jan Dhan Yojana, aimed to bring millions of unbanked Indians into the formal banking system, significantly increasing access to banking services and financial products.

Critiques and Analysis

The economic policies under Modi's leadership have not been without criticism.

The pace of economic reforms, their impact on the informal sector, and the handling of the COVID-19 economic fallout have been points of contention. Yet, a balanced perspective reveals a more nuanced understanding of Modi's financial legacy, acknowledging the intentions behind his policies and the successes achieved, even as it critically examines their limitations and the challenges that remain.

Conclusion

Narendra Modi's tenure as Prime Minister has been a period of significant economic reformation for India. His policies, characterized by bold decisions and ambitious visions, have left an indelible mark on the country's economic landscape. As we assess the impact of these reforms, it is clear that while they have propelled India towards greater financial resilience and global competitiveness, the journey is far from over. The ongoing challenges and prospects for the Indian economy suggest that Modi's economic legacy will continue to be a subject of debate and analysis for years, offering valuable lessons on the complexities of navigating economic transformation in a rapidly changing world.

Delving Deeper into GST Implementation Challenges and Adjustments

The introduction of the Goods and Services Tax (GST) in July 2017 was a landmark moment in India's economic history.

Touted as the most significant tax reform since independence, GST aimed to consolidate numerous central and state taxes into a single tax system, facilitating a unified market across the country.

However, the ambitious overhaul brought challenges, particularly for small and medium enterprises (SMEs) that found themselves grappling with the complexities of the new system.

Challenges Faced by Businesses

Significant challenges marked the transition to GST for businesses, especially SMEs. These challenges included:

Compliance Burden: The new system required businesses to file multiple monthly returns, which proved particularly onerous for smaller businesses lacking the resources to manage these requirements efficiently.

Technological Hurdles: The digital nature of GST filing demanded a level of technical access and literacy that many smaller businesses did not possess. This gap led to difficulties filing returns and accessing the GST portal, further complicating compliance.

Increased Costs: For many small businesses, the transition to GST necessitated investments in new software or professional services to manage compliance, leading to increased operational costs.

Government Adjustments and Amendments

In response to these challenges, the Indian government took several steps to ease the transition for businesses and address their concerns:

Simplification of Returns: The government introduced measures to simplify the return filing process, including the option of quarterly returns for small businesses, reducing the compliance burden.

GST Rate Adjustments: Recognizing the impact of GST rates on various sectors, the government periodically reviewed and adjusted GST rates to address sector-specific concerns and ease the tax burden on critical goods and services.

Enhanced Support and Outreach: The government ramped up its outreach and support efforts, including establishing help desks and online resources to assist businesses in navigating the new system.

Impact on the Economy

Despite initial teething problems, the GST has had a profound impact on the Indian economy:

Enhanced Tax Compliance: The streamlined tax system has improved tax compliance, significantly increasing the number of businesses registered under GST, thereby widening the tax base.

Reduction in Interstate Trade Barriers: GST has facilitated smoother interstate trade by eliminating multiple state-level taxes, thus creating a more unified national market.

Boost to Economic Efficiency: By simplifying the tax structure, GST has reduced the cascading effect of taxes, thereby making the supply chain more efficient and reducing the overall tax burden on consumers.

The journey of GST implementation in India exemplifies the complexities of large-scale economic reforms. While the initial challenges were significant, the adjustments and amendments made by the government have helped in smoothing the transition, showcasing the capacity for policy evolution in response to feedback from the business community and the broader economy. The GST's long-term impact on fostering a more efficient, transparent, and unified market is a testament to the transformative potential of well-conceived economic policies.

Banking Sector Overhaul: Focus on NPAs and Financial Inclusion Initiatives

The Indian banking sector has long been the backbone of the country's economy, facilitating growth, investment, and savings. However, the industry has also faced significant challenges, particularly in the form of non-performing assets (NPAs) and a lack of widespread financial inclusion.

Recognizing these issues, Narendra Modi's government embarked on reforms to overhaul the banking sector, address the NPA crisis, and enhance access to banking services for India's vast population.

Addressing Non-Performing Assets (NPAs)

The NPA crisis, which refers to loans or advances in default or arrears, had become a substantial burden on the Indian banking sector, particularly public sector banks. High levels of NPAs were not just a reflection of the banking sector's health but also impacted the broader economy by restricting the flow of credit to vital industries.

Insolvency and Bankruptcy Code (IBC): Introduced in 2016, the IBC was a significant step towards resolving the issue of NPAs. It provided a streamlined and time-bound process for resolving insolvency, enabling quicker recovery of stressed assets.

Recapitalization of Banks: The government announced a massive recapitalization plan for public sector banks to shore up their capital base and enable them to increase lending and support economic growth.

Asset Quality Review (AQR): Conducted by the Reserve Bank of India (RBI), the AQR aimed at cleaning up the banks' books by requiring them to recognize NPAs and make adequate provisions for them, thus reflecting a more accurate picture of their financial health.

Promoting Financial Inclusion

Alongside the efforts to clean up the banking sector, the Modi government strongly emphasized financial inclusion, aiming to bring banking services to every Indian citizen.

Pradhan Mantri Jan Dhan Yojana (PMJDY): Launched in 2014, this scheme aimed to ensure affordable access to financial services, including banking, remittance, credit, insurance, and pension.

It has been instrumental in opening millions of new bank accounts, thereby bringing previously unbanked sections of society into the formal banking system.

Aadhaar and Mobile (JAM) Trinity: Leveraging the Aadhaar unique identification number and mobile technology, the government sought to streamline financial transactions and subsidies, reduce leakage, and ensure that benefits reached the intended recipients directly.

Impact and Evaluation

The banking sector reforms have had a profound impact on the Indian economy:

Strengthening of Banks: The efforts to address NPAs and recapitalize banks have begun to bear fruit, with many banks showing improved balance sheets and reduced levels of stressed assets.

Increased Access to Banking Services: Financial inclusion initiatives have significantly increased the number of people with access to banking services, enabling them to participate more fully in the economy.

Enhanced Credit Flow: With the banking sector on firmer footing, the flow of credit to critical sectors of the economy has improved, supporting growth and development.

While challenges remain, the reforms initiated under Modi's leadership have set the stage for a more robust and inclusive banking sector in India. By addressing the twin issues of NPAs and financial exclusion, these reforms have strengthened the banking sector and contributed to the broader goal of economic empowerment and growth.

Analyzing Critiques and Balanced Perspectives on Modi's Economic Policies

Ambitious economic reforms have marked Narendra Modi's tenure as Prime Minister of India to transform the Indian economy. While these reforms have garnered praise for their boldness and vision, they have also attracted significant criticism. This section delves into the critiques and offers a balanced perspective on Modi's economic policies, considering the viewpoints of economists, business leaders, and the general populace.

Economic Criticisms

The criticisms of Modi's economic policies can be broadly categorized into concerns over implementation, impact on the informal sector, and the response to the COVID-19 pandemic.

Implementation Challenges: Critics argue that implementing critical policies like demonetization and GST was hastily done, causing unnecessary economic disruption. The demonetization initiative, in particular, is often cited as an example where the lack of planning and preparation led to widespread chaos and hardship for the common people, especially those in the informal sector.

Impact on the Informal Sector: The informal sector, which employs a significant portion of India's workforce, was hit hard by demonetization and the initial rollout of GST. Critics point to the lack of adequate support mechanisms for small businesses and informal workers during these transitions, leading to job losses and a slowdown in economic activity in this crucial segment of the economy.

COVID-19 Economic Fallout: Handling the economic fallout from the COVID-19 pandemic has also been a point of criticism.

While the government rolled out several economic relief packages, critics argue that the measures were insufficient to address the scale of the crisis, particularly for the most vulnerable sections of society.

Balanced Perspectives

While acknowledging the criticisms, it's important to offer a balanced view considering the achievements and intentions behind Modi's economic policies.

Long-term Vision: Modi's supporters of the economic agenda emphasize the long-term vision behind policies like demonetization and GST. They argue that these reforms were necessary to tackle deep-rooted issues like corruption, tax evasion, and the informal economy, setting the foundation for a more transparent, efficient, and formalized economic system.

Adaptation and Adjustments: The government's willingness to adapt and make adjustments in response to feedback, especially regarding GST, demonstrates a responsiveness to the needs of the business community and the general populace. These adjustments have helped mitigate some initial challenges and smoothed the path for greater acceptance and implementation of the reforms.

Promotion of Digital Economy and Financial Inclusion: The push towards a digital economy and financial inclusion through initiatives like the Jan Dhan Yojana and the promotion of digital payments has been widely acknowledged as a positive step towards inclusive economic growth. These initiatives have helped bring millions of Indians into the formal banking system and increased the adoption of digital transactions, contributing to economic efficiency and transparency.

Conclusion

Narendra Modi's economic policies represent a bold attempt to transform the Indian economy.

While they have faced criticism for their implementation and impact, particularly on the informal sector, it's essential to consider these reforms' broader context and long-term objectives. A balanced perspective acknowledges the challenges and critiques and recognizes these policies' achievements and potential to reshape India's economic landscape. As India continues to navigate its path of economic development, the lessons learned from these reforms will undoubtedly play a crucial role in shaping future policies and strategies.

Reflecting on Future Prospects and Ongoing Challenges for the Indian Economy Post-Reforms

As we assess the landscape of the Indian economy following a suite of significant reforms under Prime Minister Narendra Modi, it becomes imperative to look forward, considering both the opportunities and challenges that lie ahead. The economic trajectory of India, influenced heavily by policies such as demonetization, the Goods and Services Tax (GST), banking sector reforms, and initiatives aimed at financial inclusion and digitalization, suggests a complex interplay of growth potential and structural hurdles.

Future Prospects

The reforms have set the stage for a series of positive outcomes for the Indian economy:

Enhanced Global Competitiveness: India's efforts to streamline its tax system, improve ease of doing business, and foster a digital economy will likely enhance its attractiveness as a destination for foreign investment, thereby boosting its global competitiveness.

Digital Economy Expansion: The push towards digital transactions and financial services has opened new avenues for economic growth, innovation, and entrepreneurship, particularly in fintech and related sectors.

Sustainable Economic Development: Initiatives aimed at financial inclusion and the formalization of the economy are expected to contribute to more sustainable and inclusive economic development, ensuring that growth benefits a broader section of the population.

Ongoing Challenges

Despite the optimistic outlook, the Indian economy faces several ongoing challenges that could affect its future growth trajectory:

Job Creation: One of the most pressing challenges is the need for substantial job creation to accommodate the millions entering the job market each year. Addressing the issue of jobless growth and ensuring that economic expansion translates into employment opportunities will be critical.

Agricultural Sector Reforms: The agricultural sector, which employs a significant portion of India's population, requires deep reforms to improve productivity, sustainability, and profitability, ensuring food security and livelihoods for millions of rural Indians.

Navigating Global Uncertainties: The global economic environment, characterized by uncertainties such as trade tensions, climate change, and geopolitical shifts, poses challenges for India. Adapting to these changes while maintaining economic stability and growth will require agile policymaking and international cooperation.

Conclusion

The economic reforms initiated under Prime Minister Narendra Modi have undoubtedly marked a turning point for the Indian economy, addressing longstanding issues and setting the foundation for a modern, transparent, and efficient economic system. While the journey has been fraught with challenges and criticisms, the reforms have also opened up new possibilities for growth and development.

The Indian economy stands at a crossroads with significant potential for further expansion and global integration. However, realizing this potential will necessitate continued reform efforts, particularly in sectors that have yet to fully benefit from the economic changes of the past few years. It will also require a nuanced understanding of the global economic landscape and a commitment to inclusive growth that leaves no population segment behind.

As India moves forward, the lessons learned from implementing recent reforms will be invaluable in guiding future policy decisions. The path ahead is promising and challenging, requiring a balanced approach that leverages India's strengths while addressing its vulnerabilities. In this context, the economic legacy of Narendra Modi's tenure will continue to be a subject of analysis and debate, serving as a critical reference point for understanding the complexities of economic transformation in a rapidly evolving global context.

Concluding Remarks: Economic Reformation under Narendra Modi

As we conclude our exploration of the economic reformation under Prime Minister Narendra Modi, we must synthesize the key points discussed and ponder the implications for future research and policy development.

Modi's tenure has been characterized by bold and transformative economic policies, including demonetization, the implementation of the Goods and Services Tax (GST), banking sector reforms, and digitalization and financial inclusion initiatives. These measures have collectively addressed deep-rooted issues within the Indian economy, such as corruption, inefficiency, and the lack of a unified tax system.

Summary of Key Points

Demonetization and GST: While controversial, these policies aimed to curb corruption, enhance tax compliance, and unify the country's tax structure, respectively. Their implementation faced challenges, sparking debate over their short-term disruptions versus long-term economic benefits.

Banking Sector Reforms: Efforts to tackle non-performing assets and promote financial inclusion have been pivotal in strengthening the banking sector and expanding access to financial services for millions of Indians.

Economic Growth and Job Creation: Despite achieving periods of high GDP growth and increased foreign direct investment, the challenge of translating economic expansion into substantial job creation remains.

Balanced Perspectives: Critiques focus on the execution of reforms and their impact on the informal sector, while supporters highlight the long-term vision behind Modi's policies and their potential to foster a more efficient, transparent, and inclusive economy.

Implications for Future Research and Policy Development

The economic policies enacted under Modi's leadership present fertile ground for further research, particularly in assessing their long-term impact on various economic and population sectors. Future research could focus on:

Comparative Analysis: Examining the Indian experience compared to other countries that have undertaken similar economic reforms to identify best practices and lessons learned.

Sector-Specific Studies: Delve into the impact of these reforms on specific sectors, such as manufacturing, services, and agriculture, to understand their implications for growth, employment, and sustainability.

Social and Political Impacts: Investigating the broader social and political implications of economic reforms, including their effects on inequality, social mobility, and political engagement.

For policy development, the experiences gleaned from Modi's economic reforms underscore the importance of:

Inclusive Growth: Ensuring that economic policies benefit all segments of society, particularly the most vulnerable, to foster equitable growth.

Adaptability and Feedback: Policies must be adaptable and responsive to feedback from businesses, economists, and the general public to mitigate adverse impacts and enhance their effectiveness.

Sustainable Development: Balancing economic growth with environmental sustainability and resilience to global economic uncertainties.

In conclusion, the economic reformation under Narendra Modi represents a significant chapter in India's economic history.

While both achievements and challenges have marked the journey, the reforms have undeniably set the stage for future discussions on how best to navigate the complexities of economic growth and development in the 21st century.

As India continues to evolve globally, the lessons learned from these reforms will undoubtedly influence its economic policies and development strategies for years to come.

This chapter has provided a comprehensive overview of the economic reformation under Narendra Modi, aiming to offer readers valuable insights into the complexities of implementing wide-ranging economic policies in a diverse and rapidly changing nation like India.

CHAPTER 5

DIGITAL INDIA AND BEYOND

"Digital India is more than just digital connectivity;
it is a vision to transform India into
a digitally empowered society and knowledge economy."

— Narendra Modi

Assessing the transformative impact of digitalization initiatives, this chapter explores how Modi's government utilized technology to revolutionize governance, economy, and society, making strides toward a digitally empowered country.

Introduction

Setting the Stage

The Digital India initiative, a flagship program launched by the Government of India under the stewardship of Prime Minister Narendra Modi in July 2015, aimed to transform India into a digitally empowered society and knowledge economy; this ambitious project was set against a burgeoning digital landscape in India, characterized by a rapid increase in internet users, mobile connectivity, and a burgeoning IT sector.

Yet, despite these advances, vast swathes of the population remained on the periphery of the digital revolution, grappling with issues of access, literacy, and infrastructure.

Modi's Vision for Digital Transformation

Prime Minister Narendra Modi envisioned Digital India as a comprehensive framework for leveraging technology to bring about socio-economic transformation. His vision was three-pronged: to build a digital infrastructure that would serve as a utility to every citizen, to deliver governance and services on demand, and to empower citizens digitally. Modi's approach was rooted in the belief that digital technology could be a great equalizer, bridging the gap between urban and rural, rich and poor, educated and uneducated.

Core Initiatives of Digital India

Digital Infrastructure as a Utility to Every Citizen

At the heart of the Digital India initiative was the commitment to create a robust digital infrastructure accessible to every citizen, ensuring availability and access to high-speed internet as a core utility. This involved laying thousands of kilometers of fiber-optic cables to connect rural and remote areas, alongside efforts to boost mobile connectivity across the country. Projects like BharatNet aimed to connect Gram Panchayats (village councils) to the internet, envisaging a digitally connected rural India.

Governance and Services on Demand

The government sought to harness the digital revolution to make its services more accessible to citizens nationwide. This included digitizing government processes and creating online platforms, from tax filings and business registrations to passport services and social welfare schemes.

The e-Kranti program was pivotal in this regard, pushing for the electronic delivery of services to improve efficiency, transparency, and ease of business.

Digital Empowerment of Citizens

Empowering every citizen with digital access was another cornerstone of Digital India. This encompassed initiatives aimed at promoting digital literacy among the masses, ensuring that citizens had access to digital infrastructure and the skills to use it. Programs like Pradhan Mantri Gramin Digital Saksharta Abhiyan (PMGDISHA) aimed to digitally literate rural households, focusing on older people, women, and the differently-abled. Additionally, efforts to promote digital financial inclusion sought to bring the unbanked and underbanked into the formal financial system, leveraging technology to provide access to banking services, insurance, and pension facilities.

Key Projects and Achievements

Aadhaar Integration

Aadhaar, India's biometric ID system, has been a cornerstone of the Digital India initiative, serving as a pivotal tool for digital identity verification. With over a billion enrolled members, Aadhaar has facilitated many services, from opening bank accounts to securing mobile phone connections. Its integration into the digital framework has enabled direct benefit transfers (DBT), cutting down on fraud and ensuring that subsidies reach the intended recipients directly, thereby enhancing financial inclusion and governance.

Unified Payments Interface (UPI)

The Unified Payments Interface (UPI) has revolutionized the digital payments landscape in India.

Launched in 2016, UPI enables instant money transfers between bank accounts on a mobile platform, simplifying transactions and promoting a cashless economy. Its widespread adoption has fueled the growth of the fintech sector and democratized access to banking services, making digital transactions accessible to a broader segment of the population.

E-Governance Platforms

Significant strides have been made in e-governance, with platforms like MyGov, e-Hospital, and digital land records management transforming how citizens interact with the government. MyGov, a citizen engagement platform, has fostered a participatory approach to governance, allowing citizens to contribute ideas and feedback on policy and governance. E-Hospital has streamlined hospital services, enabling online registration, appointment booking, and access to medical reports. Digital land records management has improved transparency and efficiency in land-related transactions, reducing disputes and facilitating access to land records.

Impact on Society and Economy

Digital Economy Growth

The Digital India initiative has significantly contributed to the growth of India's digital economy. The proliferation of digital infrastructure, coupled with initiatives like UPI and digital identity verification through Aadhaar, has catalyzed the expansion of the e-commerce sector, digital startups, and the IT industry. This digital boom has created millions of jobs and fostered innovation, entrepreneurship, and investment in the tech sector. The rise of digital startups, in particular, has positioned India as a global hub for innovation and technology-driven enterprises.

Societal Transformation

Digital initiatives have ushered in profound societal changes, impacting how people communicate, access information, and conduct transactions.

Increased digital literacy, facilitated by government programs, has empowered citizens across diverse socio-economic backgrounds, particularly in rural and remote areas. This digital empowerment has bridged the urban-rural divide, enabling online access to education, healthcare, and government services. Furthermore, digital transformation has played a pivotal role in enhancing the participation of women and marginalized communities in the digital economy, promoting inclusivity and social equity.

Challenges and Critiques

Despite the notable achievements, the journey towards a fully digital India has challenges. The digital divide remains a significant concern, with disparities in internet access and digital literacy persisting across different regions and socio-economic groups. Privacy, data security, and surveillance issues have also emerged, particularly about the Aadhaar system and digital transactions. These concerns highlight the need for robust data protection laws and measures to ensure the privacy and security of citizens' information.

Challenges and Critiques

Digital Divide

The persistent digital divide is one of the most pressing challenges facing the Digital India initiative. Despite significant strides in expanding digital infrastructure, a substantial portion of the Indian population remains disconnected from the digital world, particularly in rural areas and among lower-income groups. The reasons range from lack of infrastructure and affordable internet access to low digital literacy. This divide impedes equitable access to digital opportunities and risks widening socio-economic disparities.

Privacy and Security Concerns

The rapid digitization of services, especially the integration of Aadhaar for identity verification and access to services, has raised significant concerns regarding privacy and data security. Critics argue that without stringent data protection laws, the accumulation of personal data by the state and corporations poses risks of surveillance and misuse. The Supreme Court of India's ruling on the right to privacy as a fundamental right under the Constitution in 2017 highlighted the need to balance digital advancements with privacy protections.

Data Localization and Regulatory Challenges

The push for data localization, requiring companies to store and process data on servers in India, has sparked debate about its implications for digital trade, innovation, and privacy. While the government advocates for data localization as necessary for national security and citizen privacy, critics argue it could impede the growth of the digital economy, affect international relations, and increase operational costs for businesses.

International Perspective and Collaboration

Global Standing

The Digital India initiative has significantly enhanced India's global standing in technology, innovation, and digital governance. By pioneering projects like Aadhaar and UPI, India has set benchmarks for digital identity verification and payment systems, attracting global attention and emulation. These achievements have positioned India as a leader in digital innovation, with countries looking to replicate similar models in their digital infrastructure development.

International Collaborations

Numerous international collaborations and partnerships have bolstered India's digital transformation journey.

These collaborations span various areas, including cybersecurity, digital infrastructure development, e-governance, and digital literacy. Partnerships with global tech giants, international organizations, and foreign governments have facilitated the exchange of technology, best practices, and resources, contributing to India's rapid growth and success in digital initiatives. For instance, collaborations with companies like Google, Microsoft, and Facebook have brought investments, technology transfers, and initiatives to improve internet connectivity, digital literacy, and innovation. Furthermore, India's active participation in international digital technology and governance forums has fostered dialogue on global digital policy issues, emphasizing the importance of inclusivity, security, and cooperation in the digital age.

Conclusion

Assessment of Digital Transformation

The Digital India initiative marks a significant milestone in India's journey towards becoming a digitally empowered society and knowledge economy. Under Prime Minister Narendra Modi's leadership, the initiative has achieved remarkable progress in building digital infrastructure, enhancing governance through technology, and empowering citizens digitally. The successes of projects like Aadhaar and UPI underscore India's capacity for digital innovation, contributing to economic growth, societal transformation, and improved governance. However, the journey is far from complete. The digital divide, privacy and security concerns, and the need for robust regulatory frameworks remain significant challenges. Addressing these issues requires a nuanced approach that balances technological advancement with the protection of citizen rights and equitable access to digital opportunities.

Future Prospects

The future of digital transformation in India is poised for further evolution. Emerging technologies such as artificial intelligence, blockchain, and the Internet of Things (IoT) offer new opportunities for innovation and development. The focus on creating a digital innovation ecosystem, fostering startups, and investing in technology education and research will be crucial for sustaining growth and competitiveness. The ongoing and future challenges for Digital India, including bridging the digital divide, ensuring data privacy, and fostering international collaboration, underscore the need for adaptive policies, inclusive strategies, and global cooperation. As India continues its digital transformation journey, the vision of a fully inclusive and digitally empowered society remains a guiding beacon.

Looking Forward

Digital India's journey reflects a transformative phase in governance, economy, and society, driven by the vision of leveraging technology for the greater good. As India navigates the evolving global digital landscape and internal demands for sustainable and inclusive digital growth, the lessons learned, and the milestones achieved offer valuable insights. The path forward, illuminated by innovation, inclusivity, and collaboration, promises to further India's digital ambitions and contribute to shaping a global digital future that benefits all.

This chapter provided a comprehensive overview of the Digital India initiative, offering insights into its impact, achievements, and future challenges. As the narrative unfolds, the transformative power of digitalization under Narendra Modi's leadership emerges as a testament to the potential for technology to drive societal change, underscoring the importance of continued innovation, inclusivity, and cooperation in the digital era.

CHAPTER 6

REVOLUTIONIZING HEALTH AND EDUCATION

"Investing in health and education is not just policy;
it's an investment in the future of India,
ensuring every citizen can achieve their full potential."

— Narendra Modi

Exploring the significant reforms in healthcare and education, this chapter highlights the initiatives aimed at uplifting India's human capital. It analyzes the policies' effectiveness and their contribution to building a more inclusive and progressive society.

Introduction

India's journey toward significant health and education reforms under Prime Minister Narendra Modi's leadership marks a pivotal chapter in the country's developmental saga. Before Modi's tenure, the landscape of Indian healthcare and education was fraught with challenges. Limited access to quality healthcare, uneven distribution of educational resources, and stark disparities in outcomes across different societal segments characterized the pre-Modi era.

The groundwork for transformative policies laid by Modi aimed to address these enduring challenges and propel India towards a future of inclusive growth and enhanced human capital development.

Pre-Modi Landscape

The state of healthcare and education in India before 2014 was a study in contrast. On one hand, India's global contributions in various fields, including technology and medicine, painted a picture of a nation on the rise. On the other hand, domestic reality told a different story. Access to healthcare was heavily skewed, with urban areas enjoying comparatively better services than their rural counterparts. The education system, while vast, often failed to meet global standards of quality and relevance, leaving a significant portion of the youth underprepared for the challenges of the modern workforce.

Vision for Reform

Narendra Modi's vision for overhauling these sectors was ambitious and comprehensive. It was rooted in the belief that a healthy and well-educated populace forms the backbone of a robust economy. The goals were clear: to ensure universal healthcare access, thereby eliminating the financial burden of medical expenses on people with low incomes, and to reform the education system in a way that not only improved outcomes but also fostered innovation, skill development, and adaptability among students. This vision was to be realized through a series of strategic reforms, including the Ayushman Bharat initiative for healthcare and the National Education Policy (NEP) 2020 for education, among others.

The chapter ahead delves deep into these reforms, exploring the intricacies of their implementation, the challenges encountered, and the impacts realized. A blend of data-driven analysis and narrative storytelling aims to comprehensively understand how these reforms have started reshaping India's health and education sectors.

Healthcare Reforms

Ayushman Bharat Initiative

Launched in 2018, the Ayushman Bharat initiative is a cornerstone of Narendra Modi's healthcare reform agenda. It is often hailed as the world's largest government-funded healthcare program, aimed at providing free health coverage to over 500 million citizens, particularly targeting the poor and vulnerable sections of society. The initiative comprises two primary components: the Pradhan Mantri Jan Arogya Yojana (PM-JAY) for health insurance and the establishment Health and Wellness Centers (HWCs) nationwide.

Launch Details and Goals: PM-JAY provides a health insurance cover of up to ₹5 lakh per family per year, covering secondary and tertiary care hospitalization without any cap on family size or age. This ambitious move sought to cover nearly 40% of India's population, addressing the dire need for affordable healthcare access and protecting millions from the financial ruin associated with medical emergencies.

Impact Analysis: The impact of Ayushman Bharat has been significant and multifaceted. Within its first year, millions of hospital treatments were authorized under the scheme, demonstrating its reach and potential to change lives. The establishment of HWCs aimed to bring healthcare services closer to the rural and underserved populations, focusing on comprehensive primary care, preventive health education, and wellness activities. Together, these components have created a more accessible and equitable healthcare system in India.

COVID-19 Response

The COVID-19 pandemic tested the resilience and adaptability of healthcare systems worldwide.

Under the ambit of Ayushman Bharat and other initiatives, India's response highlighted the country's ability to rapidly mobilize resources, innovate, and scale up healthcare infrastructure.

Vaccine Development and Rollout: India played a pivotal role in vaccine development, with the indigenous Covaxin being a testament to its capabilities in research and development. The government's vaccination strategy, prioritizing frontline workers and vulnerable populations, aimed at equitable distribution and accessibility.

Digital Initiatives for Pandemic Management: The introduction of the Aarogya Setu app and the Co-WIN platform for tracking and managing vaccine appointments showcased India's approach to leveraging technology in public health emergencies. These digital tools played crucial roles in contact tracing, health information dissemination, and vaccination process streamlining.

Infrastructure Enhancements: The pandemic accelerated the expansion of healthcare infrastructure, from the rapid setup of COVID-19 care centers to the augmentation of oxygen supplies and critical care facilities. These measures addressed the immediate crisis and contributed to long-term enhancements in healthcare capacity.

Public Health Initiatives

Beyond Ayushman Bharat, other significant public health initiatives have marked Modi's tenure. The Swachh Bharat Abhiyan (Clean India Mission), launched in 2014, aimed at promoting cleanliness, hygiene, and sanitation across India. Its impacts on public health, particularly in reducing waterborne diseases and improving public health infrastructure, underscore the interconnectedness of environmental cleanliness and health outcomes. The holistic approach to healthcare reform under Narendra Modi's leadership—from insurance coverage and primary care to emergency response and public health initiatives—illustrates a comprehensive effort to uplift India's healthcare system.

These reforms have laid the groundwork for a more inclusive, accessible, and resilient healthcare infrastructure poised to meet the challenges of the 21st century.

Education Reforms

National Education Policy (NEP) 2020

The National Education Policy (NEP) 2020, unveiled by Narendra Modi's government, represents a landmark overhaul in Indian education. Aimed at making education more holistic, flexible, multidisciplinary, aligned to the needs of the 21st century, and aimed at bringing out the unique capabilities of each student, NEP 2020 marks a significant shift from the traditional education system.

Key Features and Implementation Strategies: NEP 2020 proposes several transformative changes, including introducing a new curricular structure, the 5+3+3+4 system, replacing the 10+2 system. This structure corresponds to the ages 3–8 years (Foundational Stage), 8–11 (Preparatory Stage), 11–14 (Middle Stage), and 14–18 (Secondary Stage), ensuring a continuum in education that is more responsive to the developmental stages of a child's brain. It emphasizes early childhood care and education (ECCE), national curricular and pedagogical frameworks for early childhood education, the national mission on foundational literacy and numeracy, and no rigid separations between academic streams in secondary education.

Shifts in Pedagogical Approaches and Technology Integration: The policy advocates for active pedagogy that makes learning more engaging and enjoyable. It strongly emphasizes leveraging technology in education for teaching, learning, administration, and management. The introduction of the National Educational Technology Forum (NETF) is a step towards facilitating decision-making on the induction, deployment, and use of technology.

Digital Education Initiatives

The Modi government has accelerated its push towards digital education in response to the changing educational landscape, particularly accentuated by the COVID-19 pandemic. Initiatives like the DIKSHA platform, e-Pathshala, and Swayam have provided accessible and flexible learning options for students nationwide.

DIKSHA Platform: DIKSHA (Digital Infrastructure for Knowledge Sharing) is a national platform for school education, offering teachers, students, and parents engaging learning material relevant to the prescribed school curriculum. It supports multiple languages and is accessible on various devices, ensuring widespread reach.

E-Pathshala: Launched by the National Council of Educational Research and Training (NCERT), e-Pathshala hosts digital textbooks, audio, video, periodicals, and a variety of other print and non-print materials, making learning resources available for both students and teachers.

Swayam: SWAYAM (Study Webs of Active-Learning for Young Aspiring Minds) is an initiative designed to offer online courses in higher education to learners across India. It hosts courses taught by instructors from various Indian universities, covering a range of subjects from undergraduate to postgraduate levels.

Skill Development and Vocational Training

Complementing the educational reforms, the Skill India campaign, launched in 2015, focuses on large-scale skill development for the youth. Its objective is to enable individuals to find employment and nurture a workforce with the skills required for the evolving global market.

Skill India Campaign: It encompasses various initiatives, including the National Skill Development Mission, the Pradhan Mantri Kaushal Vikas Yojana (PMKVY), and the establishment of Industrial Training Institutes (ITIs). These programs offer vocational training and skill development courses across various sectors to bridge the gap between education and employment.

The cumulative effect of these education and skill development reforms is profound, promising to equip India's youth with the necessary skills and knowledge to thrive in the global economy. By fostering a flexible, inclusive learning environment that aligns with modern technological advancements, these reforms pave the way for a future where every citizen can contribute meaningfully to the nation's growth.

Impact and Outcomes

The ambitious reforms undertaken in healthcare and education under Narendra Modi's leadership have begun to reshape India's societal fabric. While it is still early to quantify the full spectrum of impacts, preliminary assessments suggest significant strides toward improving health outcomes, literacy rates, and skill levels among the population. However, these transformations have not been without their challenges.

Assessing the Impact on Society

Health Outcomes: The Ayushman Bharat initiative has provided millions of access to necessary healthcare services, potentially reducing mortality rates and improving public health. Initiatives like Swachh Bharat Abhiyan have contributed to decreased incidences of waterborne diseases.

Literacy and Education: NEP 2020's focus on foundational literacy and numeracy, along with its emphasis on critical thinking and flexibility, aims to improve education quality and outcomes significantly.

Digital education platforms have ensured continuity in learning amidst disruptions like the COVID-19 pandemic.

Skill Development: Skill India's efforts to bridge the gap between formal education and employment requirements have started to show promise in enhancing employability among the youth, aligning India's workforce with the demands of a global economy.

Challenges and Critiques

Despite these positive strides, the implementation of reforms faces several hurdles:

Disparities in Access: While initiatives aim for universal coverage, disparities in access to healthcare and education persist, particularly in rural and underprivileged urban areas.

Infrastructure Limitations: The ambitious scale of reforms occasionally outpaces the existing infrastructure, leading to bottlenecks in service delivery, especially in remote regions.

Digital Divide: The push towards digital education, although innovative, highlights the digital divide, with students in less affluent areas struggling to access digital resources due to a lack of devices or reliable internet.

Success Stories and Case Studies

Amidst these challenges, numerous success stories highlight the transformative potential of these reforms:

Healthcare: The story of Ayushman Bharat facilitating life-saving surgery for a farmer's daughter in rural India exemplifies the scheme's impact. The initiative's reach, covering over 50 crore beneficiaries, underscores its potential to transform healthcare accessibility.

Education: The rapid adoption of digital platforms during the pandemic, with platforms like DIKSHA seeing exponential increases in user engagement, illustrates the resilience and adaptability of India's education system.

Skill Development: Individual narratives of young adults securing employment through Skill India's vocational training programs underscore the tangible benefits of aligning education with market needs.

International Recognition and Collaboration

The reforms have not only garnered domestic acclaim but have also attracted international attention. India's COVID-19 vaccine initiative and digital health responses have been lauded globally. Similarly, NEP 2020 has sparked interest in its holistic approach to education, with several countries exploring collaborations in educational technology and policy sharing.

Conclusion

Reflecting on the journey of health and education reforms under Narendra Modi, it is evident that while significant progress has been made, the path ahead is filled with challenges. The true measure of success will be in sustaining the momentum, continuously addressing the disparities, and adapting to the evolving needs of India's population. The future of healthcare and education in India appears promising, with ongoing initiatives and potential reforms poised to transform these critical sectors further. The long-term implications of these reforms for India's development, human capital, and global standing remain a compelling narrative of growth, resilience, and inclusivity.

Future Prospects and Ongoing Initiatives

Healthcare Sector

The future of healthcare in India appears to be on a trajectory toward more inclusive, technology-driven, and preventive care models. Ongoing initiatives aim to expand the reach of Ayushman Bharat, focusing on adding more Health and Wellness Centers (HWCs) to provide comprehensive primary healthcare across the nation. Integrating digital health records as part of the National Digital Health Mission is another step forward, aiming to create a seamless online platform for citizens to access medical services and health information.

Healthcare innovation, spurred by initiatives like the Atal Innovation Mission, is expected to foster new solutions in telemedicine, digital health, and medical devices, making healthcare more accessible and affordable. The government's emphasis on increasing public health expenditure to 2.5% of GDP by 2025 reflects a commitment to further strengthening healthcare infrastructure and services.

Education Sector

The implementation of NEP 2020 continues to be a significant focus, with efforts geared towards revamping curricula, teaching methodologies, and assessment practices to make education more holistic and student-centric. The policy's emphasis on technology integration will likely see an expansion in digital learning platforms and tools, aiming to bridge the educational divide and cater to diverse learning needs. Skill development remains a priority, with the government expanding the scope of Skill India initiatives to include new-age skills like artificial intelligence, robotics, and digital marketing. Establishing more Institutes of Skill Development, in partnership with industries and international institutions, is anticipated to enhance vocational training and employability.

Long-term Implications

The long-term implications of these reforms are manifold. By elevating the standards of healthcare and education, India is poised to harness its demographic dividend more effectively, translating into economic growth and enhanced social equity. Improved health outcomes and a more educated and skilled workforce can drive innovation, increase productivity, and attract foreign investment, positioning India as a global power in the coming decades.

The journey of reforming India's healthcare and education sectors is a testament to the nation's resolve to overcome its challenges and embrace a future of prosperity and well-being. The ongoing efforts and future directions signal a commitment to continuous improvement and adaptation, reflecting a vision that extends beyond immediate gains to long-term global competitiveness and human development.

Reflecting on the transformative journey of healthcare and education reforms in India, it's clear that the path ahead is as promising as it is challenging. The lessons learned underscore the importance of resilience, innovation, and inclusivity in shaping a nation's future.

This concludes our detailed exploration of "Revolutionizing Health and Education" under Narendra Modi's leadership. The narrative woven through the reforms, impacts, challenges, and future directions offers a comprehensive view of a nation in transformation, striving to realize the full potential of its human capital.

CHAPTER 7

ENVIRONMENTAL PARADIGM SHIFT

"Our commitment to the environment goes beyond
treaties and agreements;
it is a pledge to our future generations for
a cleaner, greener, and sustainable planet."

— Narendra Modi

Evaluating India's strategies for environmental sustainability, this chapter scrutinizes the country's efforts in climate action, renewable energy adoption, and global environmental leadership, assessing the shift towards sustainable development.

Introduction

India's trajectory has been uniquely compelling in the labyrinth of global environmental governance, marked by a blend of challenges and transformative policies. Before 2014, India grappled with formidable environmental challenges, including escalating pollution levels, rampant deforestation, and the looming threats of climate change. These issues posed significant risks to India's ecological balance, socio-economic stability, public health, and cultural heritage.

The ascension of Narendra Modi to India's prime ministership in 2014 heralded a new era in the nation's approach to environmental sustainability. Modi's vision was not just a policy shift but a philosophical reorientation towards environmental stewardship, aiming to reconcile India's rapid economic growth with the imperative of ecological conservation. This vision championed the integration of traditional Indian environmental practices—rooted in a deep reverence for nature—with the precision and scalability of modern technology.

Under Modi's administration, India embarked on an ambitious journey to overhaul its environmental policies, seeking to position itself as a global leader in climate action and sustainable development. This chapter delves into the narrative arc of India's environmental paradigm shift, elucidating Modi's strategic initiatives, the challenges encountered, and the tangible impacts on both the national and global stage.

Pre-Modi Environmental Challenges

Before Narendra Modi's tenure, India's environmental landscape was characterized by daunting challenges. Air pollution in major cities frequently exceeded safe limits, with the capital, New Delhi, often shrouded in hazardous smog. Water pollution, too, was pervasive, with numerous rivers and water bodies contaminated by industrial effluents and untreated sewage, severely impacting public health and biodiversity.

Deforestation presented another critical concern, driven by urbanization, industrial expansion, and agricultural encroachment. This led to the loss of habitat for countless species and exacerbated the effects of climate change, diminishing the country's carbon sink capacity.

The socio-economic implications of these environmental challenges were profound. Climate change, manifesting in erratic weather patterns, floods, and droughts, threatened food security, livelihoods, and the well-being of millions, particularly those in vulnerable rural communities.

Modi's Environmental Vision

Narendra Modi's vision for environmental sustainability was articulated with a clear understanding of these challenges and an unwavering commitment to addressing them. His approach was predicated on the belief that economic development and environmental conservation could be mutually reinforcing rather than mutually exclusive.

Modi advocated for leveraging India's rich tradition of nature worship and sustainable living, merging these principles with cutting-edge innovation and technology. This vision aimed to foster a society where sustainable practices were not just adopted as policy measures but embedded in the collective consciousness of the citizenry.

Modi's government introduced many initiatives, policies, and international collaborations to realize this vision, targeting a comprehensive overhaul of India's environmental governance. The subsequent sections thoroughly explore these initiatives, assessing their impact and the broader implications for global environmental policy discourse.

Key Environmental Policies and Initiatives

International Solar Alliance (ISA)

One of the most groundbreaking initiatives under Narendra Modi's leadership was the formation of the International Solar Alliance (ISA) in 2015, co-founded by India and France on the sidelines of the COP21 climate conference in Paris. The ISA's primary objective is to mobilize efforts among solar resource-rich countries to harness solar energy efficiently, aiming to promote sustainable energy and reduce dependency on fossil fuels. India's role in spearheading the ISA underscores its commitment to renewable energy and positions it as a global leader in climate action.

The alliance has made significant strides, facilitating the deployment of solar technologies across member countries, fostering solar innovation, and mobilizing billions of dollars in solar financing. Projects under the ISA umbrella exemplify the potential of international cooperation in accelerating the global transition to clean energy.

Swachh Bharat Abhiyan (Clean India Mission)

Launched in 2014, the Swachh Bharat Abhiyan (SBA) or Clean India Mission represented a nationwide campaign to eliminate open defecation and improve solid waste management. Beyond its immediate objectives, the mission has profoundly impacted India's public health, sanitation, and environmental cleanliness.

The SBA's comprehensive approach, which includes constructing toilets, promoting hygiene practices, and implementing waste management systems, has significantly reduced waterborne diseases and pollution. The mission's success is a testament to the potential of large-scale public health initiatives to effect environmental change.

National Clean Air Program (NCAP)

The National Clean Air Program, launched in 2019, signifies India's targeted effort to combat air pollution. Intending to reduce particulate matter (PM) pollution by 20-30% from 2017 levels by 2024, the NCAP outlines a multi-sectoral and collaborative approach. This includes augmenting air quality monitoring networks, strengthening enforcement, and promoting cleaner production and fuel technologies.

The NCAP represents a critical component of Modi's environmental vision, addressing one of the country's most pressing environmental challenges. While progress has been incremental, the program's comprehensive framework sets a precedent for systematic action against air pollution.

Sustainable Development Goals (SDGs)

Modi's environmental initiatives demonstrate a strong alignment with the United Nations' Sustainable Development Goals, particularly those related to clean energy (SDG 7), clean water and sanitation (SDG 6), and climate action (SDG 13). The concerted efforts to expand renewable energy capacity, improve water and sanitation infrastructure, and reduce air pollution contribute directly to these global objectives.

India's progress towards the SDGs under Modi's leadership highlights the potential for national policies to address local environmental challenges and contribute to global sustainability targets. However, challenges remain, including the need for greater financial investment, technological innovation, and international collaboration to fully realize these goals.

Climate Change and International Commitments

Under Narendra Modi, India has reaffirmed its commitment to the Paris Agreement, aiming to reduce greenhouse gas emissions intensity by 33-35% from 2005 levels by 2030. India's efforts include increasing its renewable energy capacity, with ambitious solar and wind energy targets, and promoting energy efficiency across various sectors. Modi's advocacy for global climate action is evident in his active participation in international forums and calls for collective responsibility and cooperation among nations. India's leadership, particularly in initiatives like the ISA, showcases its commitment to spearheading global efforts against climate change. Under Narendra Modi's administration, India's environmental paradigm shift illustrates a comprehensive and ambitious approach to sustainability. Balancing economic development with environmental conservation, these policies and initiatives mark significant strides towards a sustainable future, with implications that resonate beyond India's borders.

Innovation and Technology in Environmental Management

Under Narendra Modi's stewardship, India has embraced digital innovations and technology as pivotal tools for environmental management. The government has launched several initiatives leveraging technology to monitor environmental quality, enhance forest cover, and conserve wildlife, illustrating a forward-thinking approach to ecological stewardship.

Digital Innovations

One notable example is satellite technology and Geographic Information Systems (GIS) for real-time monitoring of forest cover, pollution levels, and water resources. These technologies have enabled more effective policy decisions, targeted conservation efforts, and efficient resource management. Additionally, the National Clean Air Programme (NCAP) employs air quality monitoring systems to provide data-driven insights for pollution control strategies, illustrating the role of technology in addressing air pollution.

Renewable Energy Projects

The shift towards renewable energy is at the heart of India's environmental transformation. Significant investments in solar and wind energy projects have been made to increase the share of renewables in India's energy mix. The government's push for solar energy, highlighted by the establishment of the International Solar Alliance (ISA), has facilitated the launch of ambitious projects like the Pavagada Solar Park in Karnataka, one of the largest solar parks in the world. These initiatives contribute to reducing India's carbon footprint and exemplify the role of innovation and technology in driving environmental sustainability. The focus on renewable energy projects underscores India's commitment to sustainable development and its role as a leader in the global transition to clean energy.

Critiques and Counterpoints

While Narendra Modi's environmental policies have been lauded for their ambition and scope, they have not been without criticism. Critics argue that some large-scale infrastructure projects have been pursued at the expense of environmental conservation, highlighting conflicts between development objectives and ecological sustainability.

Balancing Development and Environment

Balancing rapid economic development with environmental conservation remains a contentious issue. Critics point to projects that have led to deforestation and loss of biodiversity, calling for more stringent environmental impact assessments and greater transparency in project planning.

Stakeholder Engagement

The perspectives of environmental activists, local communities, and international critics on Modi's environmental policies vary widely. Some applaud the initiatives for their bold vision and positive impact, while others call for more inclusive decision-making processes that consider the voices of those directly affected by environmental policies. The engagement of stakeholders, particularly local communities, in conservation efforts and policy formulation is seen as crucial for the long-term success of India's environmental agenda.

Conclusion: Assessment of the Environmental Paradigm Shift

Under Narendra Modi's leadership, the environmental paradigm shift represents a significant transformation in India's sustainability and climate action approach. By integrating traditional values with modern technological practices, Modi's policies have set India on a path toward environmental stewardship and sustainable development.

Future Prospects

The future of India's environmental policies will likely focus on enhancing innovation, fostering international cooperation, and engaging communities more deeply in sustainability efforts. The continued integration of technology in environmental management and a commitment to renewable energy holds promise for advancing India's sustainability goals.

Legacy and Global Impact

Narendra Modi's environmental initiatives have the potential to leave a lasting legacy on India's ecological and economic landscape, contributing to global efforts to combat climate change. The balance between traditional practices and modern sustainability measures under Modi's leadership offers a model for other nations striving to achieve economic growth without compromising environmental integrity. In conclusion, while challenges remain, the environmental paradigm shift in India marks a pivotal moment in the country's journey towards sustainable development, with implications that extend beyond its borders, contributing to global environmental governance and climate action efforts.

CHAPTER 8

A NEW ERA OF DEFENSE AND DIPLOMACY

*"India's defense and diplomacy are not just about asserting power
but about forging partnerships for
peace, stability, and prosperity in the world."*

— Narendra Modi

Examining the strategic shifts in defense and foreign policy under Modi's leadership, this chapter discusses India's approach to securing its borders, enhancing its defense capabilities, and navigating the complex web of international relations.

Introduction: Crafting the opening segment with historical context and Modi's strategic vision.

Before Narendra Modi's ascent to power in 2014, India's defense and diplomatic posture was characterized by a cautious approach, often reactive rather than proactive. The nation's defense strategy was largely focused on maintaining a status quo, with sporadic efforts towards modernization hampered by bureaucratic delays and a complex procurement process. Diplomatically, India maintained a non-aligned stance, engaging with global powers on a need-based framework without overtly aligning with any.

While maintaining India's sovereignty in global affairs, this approach often limited its influence on the international stage. The election of Narendra Modi as Prime Minister marked the beginning of a new era in Indian defense and foreign policy. Modi's strategic vision was clear from the outset: to reposition India as a formidable global player regarding economic growth, defense capabilities, and diplomatic influence. This vision was rooted in a belief that a strong military and assertive diplomacy was essential for India's rise as a global power and for securing its interests against a backdrop of regional tensions and global uncertainties. A few key themes characterized Modi's approach to defense and diplomacy:

Modernization and Self-reliance: Recognizing the need to update India's aging military hardware and reduce dependence on foreign arms, Modi pushed for accelerated modernization of armed forces. The 'Make in India' initiative, aimed at boosting domestic manufacturing, was extended to the defense sector, encouraging indigenous production of defense equipment.

Proactive Diplomacy: Modi's foreign policy shifted from passive engagement to active and strategic diplomacy. High-profile visits to countries worldwide, from the United States to the Middle East and Europe to East Asia, were aimed at strengthening bilateral relations, attracting investment, and positioning India as a key player in global affairs.

Strategic Partnerships: Under Modi, India sought to deepen its strategic partnerships with major powers and regional allies. This involved defense and security collaborations and economic and technological cooperation to enhance India's capabilities and influence. This introduction sets the stage for a detailed examination of the transformative policies and governance strategies that have marked the Modi era, focusing on defense and diplomacy.

The subsequent sections will delve into the specifics of military modernization, key diplomatic engagements, and the strategic shifts that have defined India's new approach to its role on the global stage.

Defense Reforms and Modernization

Dive into the initiatives for military modernization, including procurement policies and technological advancements.

Under Narendra Modi's leadership, India embarked on an ambitious journey to overhaul its defense capabilities, a cornerstone of its broader strategy to assert itself as a global power. This journey was marked by significant reforms aimed at modernizing the military, enhancing indigenous defense production, and embracing cutting-edge technologies.

Military Modernization

The military modernization process in India under Modi has been comprehensive, targeting all branches of the armed forces with an emphasis on increasing operational readiness, strategic mobility, and firepower. Key initiatives included procuring new fighter jets, submarines, and missile systems and upgrading existing assets to extend their service life and enhance their capabilities. The government streamlined the defense procurement process to reduce delays, introducing a new policy prioritizing indigenization and transparency.

One of the landmark deals in this era was the acquisition of the Rafale jets from France, aimed at bolstering the Indian Air Force's capabilities. Similarly, the Navy's strength was augmented through the induction of the INS Kalvari, the first of the Scorpene-class submarines, significantly enhancing India's undersea warfare capability.

Indigenous Defense Production

The 'Make in India' initiative received a significant push in the defense sector, with the government encouraging both public and private enterprises to engage in defense manufacturing. This was not just about reducing reliance on imports but also about positioning India as a defense exporter. Establishing two defense industrial corridors in Uttar Pradesh and Tamil Nadu aimed to create an ecosystem supporting the defense manufacturing infrastructure.

The indigenously developed Tejas Light Combat Aircraft is a testament to India's growing prowess in defense technology. Designed by the Aeronautical Development Agency and produced by Hindustan Aeronautics Limited, the Tejas represents India's ambitions for self-reliance in defense production.

Nuclear and Space Assets

India's strategic capabilities were further enhanced through developments in its nuclear deterrence and space defense initiatives. The successful Anti-Satellite (ASAT) missile test under Mission Shakti demonstrated India's capabilities in space warfare, joining an elite group of nations with such technology. This was complemented by the continued development of India's nuclear arsenal, focusing on second-strike capabilities to strengthen its deterrence posture.

These reforms and initiatives reflect a significant shift in India's defense strategy, moving from a historically import-dependent stance to a more balanced approach emphasizing self-reliance, technological advancement, and strategic partnerships. The next sections will explore how these military advancements have been complemented by key diplomatic engagements and a focus on counterterrorism and security, further solidifying India's position on the global stage.

Key Diplomatic Engagements: Analyze India's strategic diplomatic moves and partnerships under Modi's tenure.

Narendra Modi's tenure as Prime Minister of India has been marked by a proactive and strategic approach to diplomacy to enhance India's global standing and secure its strategic interests. India has sought to strengthen its ties with neighboring countries, major powers, and strategic partners worldwide through a series of key diplomatic engagements. These efforts have been guided by a clear vision to position India as a pivotal player in global affairs, emphasizing security, economic growth, and technological collaboration.

Neighborhood First Policy

At the heart of Modi's foreign policy has been the "Neighborhood First" initiative, which prioritizes strengthening relationships with countries in the South Asian region. This policy has been instrumental in fostering a sense of regional solidarity and cooperation, addressing mutual security concerns, and enhancing economic integration. Early in his tenure, high-level visits to countries like Bangladesh, Nepal, Sri Lanka, and Bhutan underscored Modi's importance on these relationships. Through bilateral agreements, development aid, and connectivity projects, India has sought to reaffirm its role as a regional leader and a reliable partner.

One of the notable successes of this policy has been the resolution of longstanding issues, such as the land boundary agreement with Bangladesh, which resolved a decades-old border dispute. Additionally, India's efforts to promote regional connectivity and economic integration through initiatives like the BBIN (Bangladesh, Bhutan, India, Nepal) Motor Vehicles Agreement reflect its commitment to the prosperity and stability of the South Asian region.

Act East Policy

Expanding beyond its immediate neighborhood, the "Act East" policy represents India's strategic pivot towards East Asia and the broader Indo-Pacific region. This policy builds on the "Look East" policy but increasingly emphasizes security cooperation, economic partnership, and cultural ties. Modi's visits to countries like Japan, South Korea, and Australia and his participation in ASEAN and East Asia Summits have been pivotal in enhancing India's engagement with the region. The Act East policy is also seen as a counterbalance to China's growing influence, with India positioning itself as a key player in the Indo-Pacific's security architecture through strategic partnerships and defense collaborations.

Engagement with Major Powers

India's diplomatic engagements under Modi have not been limited to its neighborhood or the Indo-Pacific. The country has sought to deepen its strategic partnerships with major global powers, including the United States, Russia, and Europe. The strengthening of the India-U.S. relationship has been highlighted, with both nations elevating their partnership to a "Comprehensive Global Strategic Partnership." This relationship has seen significant cooperation in defense, counterterrorism, and economic sectors, alongside a shared vision for a free and open Indo-Pacific.

Similarly, India's ties with Russia have remained robust, underscored by defense and energy cooperation, despite India's growing closeness with the U.S. The annual India-Russia summit has continued to be a cornerstone of this enduring partnership.

Engagement with European countries, particularly France and Germany, has also seen a new dynamism, with collaborations extending beyond trade to encompass climate change, technology, and defense.

These diplomatic endeavors reflect Modi's strategic vision of using diplomacy as a tool for national development and security. By strengthening bilateral and multilateral partnerships, India under Modi has enhanced its global stature and secured key trade, technology, and security interests.

Counterterrorism and Security

Explore India's strategies and actions to enhance its security posture and counterterrorism capabilities.

In the realm of counterterrorism and security, the Modi administration has implemented a multifaceted approach that underscores India's commitment to national and regional stability. These strategies are characterized by a combination of robust internal security measures, proactive counterterrorism efforts, and strategic border management, all aimed at safeguarding the country's sovereignty and ensuring the safety of its citizens.

Domestic and International Counterterrorism Efforts

India's counterterrorism strategy under Narendra Modi has emphasized a zero-tolerance policy towards terrorism. Domestically, this has involved strengthening the legal and institutional framework to combat terrorism, including the amendment of the Unlawful Activities (Prevention) Act (UAPA) to provide law enforcement agencies with more power to deal with suspected terrorists and their financiers.

Internationally, India has actively sought to build global consensus against terrorism, leading initiatives at forums such as the United Nations to advocate for comprehensive international strategies to combat terrorism, including addressing its financing and cross-border movements.

High-level engagements with countries like the United States, Russia, and Israel have also facilitated enhanced cooperation in counterterrorism, including intelligence sharing, joint exercises, and access to advanced counterterrorism technologies and methods.

Border Security and Management

India has significantly emphasized strengthening its border security and management with challenging borders, especially with Pakistan and China. This has involved infrastructure development, technological advancements, and increased military vigilance. The construction of new border roads, fencing, and surveillance systems has been accelerated to enhance situational awareness and response capabilities.

In response to the persistent threats along the Line of Control (LoC) with Pakistan and the Line of Actual Control (LAC) with China, India has deployed additional troops and advanced military assets, including surveillance drones and missile systems. These measures have been complemented by diplomatic efforts to de-escalate tensions and resolve disputes through negotiations, albeit with mixed results.

Humanitarian and Disaster Relief

India's role in international humanitarian missions and disaster relief operations under Modi's leadership further illustrates its commitment to global solidarity and responsibility. The country has participated in numerous international disaster relief operations, providing aid and assistance to countries hit by natural disasters. The deployment of the Indian Navy for evacuation operations in Yemen and assisting Nepal following the devastating earthquake in 2015 are notable examples of India's humanitarian outreach.

These efforts underscore India's capabilities and willingness to assist in global crises and enhance its diplomatic relations and standing on the international stage.

Conclusion and Future Directions

The strategic shifts in defense and diplomatic strategies under Narendra Modi's leadership have profoundly impacted India's global standing and security posture. India has positioned itself as a more assertive and influential global player through military modernization, proactive diplomacy, and robust security measures.

The trends suggest a continued focus on enhancing military capabilities, deepening strategic partnerships, and playing a more active role in regional and global security affairs. The challenges ahead, including managing complex relationships with major powers and addressing regional security issues, will require India to navigate a delicate balance between assertiveness and diplomacy.

The legacy of these transformative years under Modi's leadership will likely be a more confident India, poised to lead in shaping the future of global geopolitics and security.

Reflecting on the insights provided in this chapter, "A New Era of Defense and Diplomacy," it's clear that under Prime Minister Narendra Modi's leadership, India has undergone significant transformations in its defense capabilities and diplomatic engagements. These changes not only redefine India's position on the global stage but also set a new course for its future international relations and security strategy.

The emphasis on military modernization and the push towards self-reliance in defense production marks a pivotal shift from India's dependence on foreign arms. The indigenous development of military assets, such as the Tejas fighter jet, and the strategic acquisitions, like the Rafale jets from France, showcase India's commitment to enhancing its defense capabilities. Furthermore, the advancements in nuclear and space assets underline India's aspirations to be a leading power with comprehensive strategic capabilities.

Modi's tenure has diplomatically seen India adopting a more assertive and proactive stance. The "Neighborhood First" and "Act East" policies, alongside strategic partnerships with global powers, reflect a nuanced approach to diplomacy, balancing traditional ties with new alliances.

These diplomatic efforts are about security and economic and technological cooperation, aiming to position India as a key player in the emerging global order.

The counterterrorism measures and border security management efforts highlight India's resolve to protect its sovereignty and ensure the safety of its citizens. The international humanitarian missions further demonstrate India's commitment to global solidarity, enhancing its image as a responsible global actor.

Future Implications for India's Global Role

The strategies and policies implemented under Modi's leadership will likely have lasting implications for India's role in global geopolitics. As India continues to enhance its military capabilities and expand its diplomatic reach, it will increasingly be seen as a pivotal player in addressing global challenges, from security to climate change.

The balance India manages to strike between growing its defense capabilities and fostering diplomatic ties will be crucial in navigating the complex dynamics of international relations.

The challenge will be maintaining strategic autonomy while deepening alliances, especially given the geopolitical tensions in the Indo-Pacific region and India's desire to play a more significant role in global governance. India's approach to counterterrorism border security and its contributions to international peacekeeping and humanitarian efforts will further define its standing as a responsible global power committed to international law and mutual respect.

Conclusion

In sum, the chapter on "A New Era of Defense and Diplomacy" portrays a nation in transition, actively seeking to redefine its place in the world.

Narendra Modi's legacy, characterized by a blend of assertive diplomacy and strategic military modernization, sets the stage for India's future endeavors on the global stage.

As India continues to navigate the challenges and opportunities of the 21st century, its actions will significantly impact global geopolitics and security.

PART III:
CULTURAL AND SOCIETAL EVOLUTION

"Our diversity is the identity of our strong democracy. It is our strength."
— Narendra Modi

CHAPTER 9

NAVIGATING THE SOCIAL MOSAIC

"India's diversity is its greatest strength,
and our culture of unity in diversity is the model
we present to the world."

— Narendra Modi

This chapter provides insights into Modi's impact on India's social fabric, exploring welfare schemes, social justice initiatives, and the challenges of governing a diverse and pluralistic society.

Introduction

Before Narendra Modi's tenure as Prime Minister, India's social fabric was a complex tapestry woven with diverse threads of culture, religion, economic status, and social norms. The nation, home to over a billion people, faced significant challenges regarding social welfare, disparities in wealth and access to resources, communal tensions, and the struggle to maintain social harmony amidst diversity. These issues were compounded by a bureaucratic system that often slowed the implementation of necessary reforms and initiatives aimed at social welfare and justice.

In 2014, Narendra Modi assumed office with a vision that promised economic revitalization and a profound emphasis on social harmony, inclusive growth, and justice for India's marginalized and underserved communities. His vision was rooted in the belief that for India to truly rise as a global power, it must first address the deep-seated issues within its societal structure—issues that hindered the nation's progress economically and socially.

Modi's approach to fostering social harmony was multifaceted, focusing on bridging the gap between the different strata of Indian society through a series of ambitious welfare schemes and social justice initiatives. These policies were aimed at addressing the longstanding disparities and creating an environment where every citizen could have the opportunity to thrive.

From financial inclusion and sanitation to gender equality and digital access, the breadth of these initiatives was vast, each targeting specific areas of need within the societal mosaic of India.

The chapter explores these initiatives in detail, examining their impact and understanding how they have contributed to the transformation of India's social dynamics. It aims to provide a comprehensive overview of the shifts observed in the societal fabric of India under Modi's leadership, highlighting not just the successes but also the challenges and criticisms that have surfaced along the way.

This exploration is not just a recounting of policies and their outcomes but also an attempt to capture the essence of India's ongoing journey toward social harmony and justice. Through this detailed introduction, we set the stage for a deeper dive into the specific initiatives and their role in navigating the complex social mosaic of contemporary India.

Welfare Schemes and Social Justice Initiatives

Under Narendra Modi's leadership, a series of welfare schemes and social justice initiatives were launched to transform India's socio-economic landscape. These initiatives were designed to address various challenges faced by the nation's populace, from financial exclusion and lack of sanitation facilities to energy poverty and gender inequality. This section delves into three key programs: the Pradhan Mantri Jan Dhan Yojana, Swachh Bharat Abhiyan, and Ujjwala Yojana, exploring their impact and the broader societal implications of these efforts.

Pradhan Mantri Jan Dhan Yojana (PMJDY)

Launched on August 28, 2014, the Pradhan Mantri Jan Dhan Yojana aimed to ensure affordable access to financial services such as banking/savings and deposit accounts, remittance, credit, insurance, and pensions. Recognizing the critical role of financial inclusion in economic empowerment, PMJDY sought to connect India's unbanked population with the formal banking system.

By March 2021, the scheme had opened over 400 million bank accounts, demonstrating its significant impact in bringing the marginalized sections of society into the economic mainstream.

Swachh Bharat Abhiyan (Clean India Mission)

The Swachh Bharat Abhiyan, launched on October 2, 2014, marked a nationwide campaign to clean up the streets, roads, and infrastructure of India's cities, towns, and rural areas, aiming to eliminate open defecation and improve solid waste management; this mission has enhanced sanitation and hygiene practices nationwide. By focusing on constructing toilets, promoting hygiene education, and encouraging healthy sanitation practices, the campaign has contributed to a perceptible improvement in public health and environmental cleanliness.

Ujjwala Yojana

The Ujjwala Yojana, launched on May 1, 2016, aimed to safeguard the health of women and children by providing them with clean cooking fuel, specifically liquefied petroleum gas (LPG), thus preventing the health hazards associated with traditional cooking methods that use polluting fuels. By March 2019, the scheme had provided over 80 million LPG connections to below-poverty-line (BPL) households, significantly reducing the incidence of respiratory diseases caused by indoor air pollution and empowering women by saving them time and effort in fuel collection and cooking.

Each of these initiatives represents a facet of Modi's comprehensive approach to addressing the diverse challenges faced by India's population. These schemes have aimed at immediate benefits and long-term societal transformation by focusing on financial inclusion, sanitation, and health. They reflect an understanding that true social change requires addressing basic needs and creating a foundation upon which further economic and social development can be built.

The impact of these initiatives extends beyond mere numbers; they have catalyzed shifts in social norms and behaviors, contributing to a broader movement towards inclusivity, health, and empowerment.

However, the journey is not without its challenges. Implementation hurdles, sustainability concerns, and the need for ongoing engagement with the beneficiary communities are critical considerations as these initiatives move forward.

Through these efforts, Modi's governance has navigated the intricate social mosaic of India, striving to stitch together a narrative of progress and inclusivity. The following sections will delve deeper into the empowerment and inclusivity efforts and address the complexities of caste and communal dynamics within the broader context of Modi's social justice initiatives.

Empowerment and Inclusivity

Empowerment and inclusivity have been central themes in Narendra Modi's approach to societal transformation in India. Through targeted initiatives, the government has sought to uplift marginalized communities, bridge gender gaps, and ensure digital access to all segments of society. This section explores two pivotal programs: the Beti Bachao, Beti Padhao campaign, and digital inclusion initiatives, shedding light on their objectives, achievements, and broader implications for societal change.

Beti Bachao, Beti Padhao (Save the Girl Child, Educate the Girl Child)

Launched in January 2015, the Beti Bachao, Beti Padhao (BBBP) campaign aimed to address the declining child sex ratio and empower girl children through education. This initiative focused on multi-sectoral interventions in critical districts with low child-sex ratios, combining awareness campaigns with welfare schemes to protect and promote the rights of girls. By emphasizing the importance of education for girls and advocating against the practice of female foeticide, **BBBP** has contributed to increased awareness and shifting societal attitudes toward gender equality. Success stories, including improved sex ratios and higher enrollment rates for girls in schools, underscore the campaign's impact on fostering a more inclusive society.

Digital Inclusion Initiatives

Recognizing the transformative power of digital technology, Modi's government has prioritized digital literacy and access through various initiatives, aiming to bridge the digital divide and empower rural and marginalized communities. Programs like Digital India, launched in July 2015, have focused on ensuring government services are available to citizens electronically, improving online infrastructure, and increasing internet connectivity.

These efforts have facilitated a surge in digital literacy, enabling access to education, healthcare, and financial services for those previously excluded. By democratizing access to information and technology, these initiatives have played a crucial role in leveling the playing field for all segments of Indian society.

The Beti Bachao, Beti Padhao campaign and digital inclusion initiatives reflect a strategic approach to empowerment and inclusivity, targeting fundamental barriers to equality and access. While significant progress has been made, these efforts highlight the ongoing need for focused interventions to address deep-rooted societal biases and infrastructural gaps. The success of these programs lies not just in their immediate outcomes but in their ability to catalyze long-term societal shifts towards greater inclusivity and empowerment.

As we move forward, addressing caste and communal dynamics remains a critical challenge in India's social fabric. The next section will explore how Modi's governance has approached these complex issues, seeking to foster unity and harmony in a diverse and multi-ethnic society.

Addressing Caste and Communal Dynamics

In navigating India's complex social mosaic, addressing the deeply entrenched caste and communal dynamics has been a significant aspect of Narendra Modi's governance. Efforts to promote social justice and equity have been reflected in policies and programs specifically designed for Scheduled Castes (SC), Scheduled Tribes (ST), Other Backward Classes (OBC), and minority communities.

Additionally, initiatives aimed at fostering interfaith harmony and managing India's diverse religious landscape have been integral to Modi's approach to social cohesion. This section examines the strategies deployed to uplift marginalized communities and the challenges in promoting communal harmony.

Policies for Scheduled Castes/Tribes and Other Backward Classes

The Modi government has implemented several policies aimed at the socio-economic development of SC, ST, and OBC communities. These include enhanced access to education through scholarships, reservations in educational institutions and government jobs, and financial inclusion initiatives to support entrepreneurship among these communities. For instance, the Stand-Up India scheme, launched in April 2016, aims to support entrepreneurship among women and SC/ST entrepreneurs by facilitating loans to set up businesses. Such policies seek to level the playing field and provide opportunities for historically marginalized groups to advance economically and socially.

Interfaith and Communal Relations

Managing India's diverse religious landscape presents unique challenges, requiring a delicate balance between respecting religious freedoms and ensuring communal harmony. Modi's government has undertaken various initiatives to promote interfaith dialogue and celebrate the pluralistic nature of Indian society. Events like International Yoga Day and the promotion of shared cultural heritage aim to transcend religious divides and foster a sense of national unity. However, the government's approach has not been without controversy, with critics pointing to instances of communal tension and alleging biases in policy implementation.

The efforts to address caste and communal dynamics in India are ongoing and complex, involving policy interventions and attempts to shift societal attitudes and norms.

While progress has been made in some areas, the path toward complete social justice and harmony is fraught with challenges, including resistance to change, political polarization, and the need for continued dialogue and reconciliation among diverse community groups.

The initiatives to empower marginalized communities and promote communal harmony are critical to the broader societal transformation envisioned under Modi's leadership. As we progress towards a conclusion, it becomes essential to assess these social policies' impact critically, engage with critiques and debates, and reflect on the shifts in India's social dynamics that have unfolded over the years.

Critiques and Societal Debates

The initiatives and policies implemented under Narendra Modi's leadership have not been without their critics and are the subject of intense societal debates. These discussions have centered on the efficacy, reach, and unintended consequences of the government's social policies. This section delves into the major critiques and the ongoing debates around social justice and equity in India, offering insights into the complexities of enacting widespread societal change.

Criticism of Social Policies

Critics of Modi's social policies argue that despite the ambitious scope of welfare schemes, there are significant gaps in their implementation and accessibility. Concerns have been raised about the inclusivity of these initiatives, with some suggesting that marginalized communities are still left behind due to systemic barriers and bureaucratic inefficiencies. For instance, while the Jan Dhan Yojana has successfully opened millions of bank accounts, there are questions about the active usage of these accounts and the actual reach of financial benefits to the poorest citizens.

Additionally, initiatives like the Swachh Bharat Abhiyan, though widely praised for their impact on sanitation and public health, have faced scrutiny over the sustainability of the behavior changes they seek to promote and the adequacy of infrastructure to support these changes long-term.

Debates on Social Justice and Equity

The ongoing debates around social justice and equity in India reflect broader questions about the effectiveness of welfare schemes in addressing deep-rooted societal issues. While the government's efforts to promote digital literacy and empower women and marginalized communities have been acknowledged, there is an ongoing discussion about whether these measures are sufficient to overcome historical inequalities and ensure equitable opportunities for all Indians.

Critiques also extend to handling caste and communal relations, with some arguing that more must be done to bridge divides and foster genuine interfaith and inter-caste harmony. Balancing majority and minority interests, ensuring fair representation and protection for all religious and social groups, and combating prejudice remain significant hurdles in India's path toward a more inclusive society.

Despite these critiques, it is essential to recognize the complexities of governing a diverse and populous nation like India. The debates signify a vibrant democracy at work, where policies and initiatives are continually scrutinized, evaluated, and discussed. This dynamic process is crucial for the evolution of social policies that are more inclusive, effective, and reflective of the needs of all segments of society.

As we assess the broader impact of Modi's policies on societal transformation, it becomes clear that while significant strides have been made, the journey towards social harmony and equity is ongoing. The final section of this chapter will evaluate the cumulative impact of these efforts on India's social fabric, considering both the achievements and the challenges that lie ahead.

Impact on Society

The cumulative impact of Narendra Modi's policies on India's social fabric is a mosaic of transformative changes, marked improvements in individual and community well-being, and ongoing challenges in bridging the deep-rooted societal divides. This section evaluates the broader societal transformation spurred by initiatives under Modi's leadership, drawing upon case studies, success stories, and the evolving dynamics of India's social landscape.

Societal Transformation and Norm Shifts

Modi's tenure has witnessed significant societal norms and behavior shifts, particularly in financial inclusion, digital literacy, sanitation, and women's empowerment. For instance, the Pradhan Mantri Jan Dhan Yojana has connected millions to the banking system and fostered a culture of savings and financial planning among the previously unbanked population. Similarly, the Swachh Bharat Abhiyan has raised public awareness about hygiene and sanitation, leading to notable improvements in public health and cleanliness.

The Ujjwala Yojana and Beti Bachao, Beti Padhao campaign have contributed to altering societal perceptions regarding women's roles and rights, promoting gender equality, and empowering women through education and better health care. These initiatives, among others, have catalyzed a shift towards a more inclusive and equitable society, although the pace and extent of change vary across different regions and communities.

Case Studies and Success Stories

Tangible improvements in individual and community well-being provide compelling evidence of the impact of Modi's social policies.

Case studies of villages declared open defecation free, stories of women entrepreneurs enabled by Stand-Up India, and narratives of young girls pursuing education and careers, previously unthinkable, highlight the positive outcomes of these initiatives. Such success stories underscore the potential of targeted social policies to bring about significant changes in the lives of millions.

Reflecting on Social Dynamics

Reflecting on the shifts in India's social dynamics under Modi, it is evident that blending traditional values with modern social policies has been challenging and enriching. While some policies have been met with resistance, others have been embraced, leading to progressive changes in societal attitudes and behaviors. The journey towards social harmony and equity is ongoing, with the need for continuous engagement, adaptation, and innovation in policy-making to address the evolving needs of India's diverse population.

Conclusion

Navigating the complex social mosaic of India requires a nuanced understanding of its diverse realities and a commitment to fostering inclusivity and justice. Narendra Modi's tenure has been characterized by ambitious efforts to transform the social landscape, achieving notable successes while facing significant challenges. The balance between traditional values and the aspirations for a modern, equitable society is delicate, necessitating thoughtful policies and societal engagement. As India continues, the challenges and opportunities ahead are immense. The role of future policies, societal engagement, and the collective will of the Indian people will be crucial in shaping the nation's social fabric. The journey towards a more inclusive, equitable, and harmonious India is a shared endeavor, requiring the collaboration of government, civil society, and communities nationwide.

This chapter has sought to examine the social changes and initiatives under Narendra Modi's leadership, highlighting the interplay between government policies and the diverse realities of India's societal fabric.

As we look to the future, the lessons learned, and the successes achieved offer valuable insights for navigating the complex social dynamics of India and any nation striving toward social harmony and equity.

CHAPTER 10

REDEFINING NATIONAL IDENTITY

"Our national identity is carved from the values of democracy, diversity, and tolerance.
This is the India we cherish and strive to strengthen."

— Narendra Modi

Discussion on cultural nationalism, its resurgence under Modi, and its effects on India's pluralistic society are explored. The chapter assesses how Modi's policies and rhetoric have influenced India's national identity and cultural cohesion.

Introduction

The chapter begins by navigating the intricate tapestry of India's national identity, tracing its origins to the independence era. India, a mosaic of diverse cultures, languages, and religions, has always been celebrated for its commitment to secularism, democracy, and pluralism. These foundational values, enshrined in the Indian Constitution, have guided the nation's ethos, promoting unity amidst diversity. This section sets the stage for understanding the complex dynamics of national identity in India, providing a backdrop against which the resurgence of cultural nationalism under Narendra Modi's leadership can be examined.

Narendra Modi's ascent to power in 2014 marked a pivotal shift in India's national identity narrative. Modi, a figure who has often been synonymous with a brand of cultural nationalism deeply rooted in Hindu cultural heritage, has envisioned an India where this form of nationalism serves as a unifying force, ostensibly strengthening the nation's fabric. This vision, however, is not without its controversies and complexities. The introduction lays out Modi's perspective on nationalism, underlining its significance in his political rhetoric and policy-making, and primes the reader for a deeper exploration of how this vision impacts India's pluralistic society.

This initial exploration into the historical context and Modi's vision sets the tone for the discussion. It aims to engage readers by presenting a nuanced view of India's national identity evolution, highlighting the tension between maintaining India's cherished pluralism and the push for a more singular cultural nationalism.

Key Policies and Statements Detail

Under Narendra Modi's leadership, policies, public statements, and initiatives have underscored the government's emphasis on cultural nationalism. This section delves into the specifics of these policies and their implications for India's national identity narrative.

One of the hallmark policies has been the promotion of the Hindi language and Sanskrit, aiming to reinforce these languages' status in the national consciousness. Efforts to integrate these languages more deeply into the education system and government functions are often cited as attempts to prioritize Hindu cultural heritage. Additionally, the government has embarked on high-profile projects to renovate and highlight Hindu religious sites, further amplifying the message of Hindu cultural primacy.

These moves, coupled with Modi's frequent invocation of Hindu mythology and symbolism in his speeches, paint a picture of a government keen on embedding Hindu cultural nationalism within the fabric of Indian society.

The revision of school textbooks to include more content on ancient Hindu scriptures and figures, as well as the portrayal of historical events from a perspective that critics argue is skewed towards a Hindu nationalist narrative, has sparked considerable debate. Some view these educational reforms as an effort to reshape the historical narrative to align with the cultural nationalism agenda.

Public statements by government officials, including Modi himself, often emphasize themes of Hindu heritage and its central role in India's identity. For instance, Modi's reference to the citizens of India as "1.3 billion Indians" who are the "bearers of a 5,000-year-old civilization" underscores this focus on ancient Hindu civilization as the cornerstone of national identity.

This detailed examination of key policies and statements reveals the multifaceted approach taken by Modi's government to promote cultural nationalism. It sets the stage for analyzing the societal impact of these measures, illustrating how they have been received by various segments of the Indian populace and the broader implications for India's pluralistic society.

Impact on Society Detail

The societal impact of Narendra Modi's push for cultural nationalism has been profound and multifaceted, engendering a wide array of responses across the diverse tapestry of Indian society. This section explores the varied reactions, from enthusiastic support to critical opposition, and the nuances in between, illuminating the complex interplay between cultural nationalism and societal dynamics.

Support from Various Segments of Society: Many have embraced the emphasis on Hindu cultural heritage, viewing it as a long-overdue acknowledgment of India's majority religion's historical and cultural significance. This sentiment is particularly strong among segments of the population who feel that previous governments have neglected Hindu heritage in favor of a more secular approach. Modi's policies represent a restoration of national pride and identity for these individuals, with large-scale projects like the construction of the Ram Temple in Ayodhya epitomizing this revival.

Criticism from Others: However, this push has also encountered substantial criticism, especially from those who argue that it undermines India's secular foundations and marginalizes non-Hindu communities. Critics contend that the emphasis on a singular cultural identity is antithetical to India's pluralistic ethos, fostering divisions and heightening communal tensions in some areas. Incidents of violence against minority communities, particularly Muslims, have been cited as examples of the societal fallout from this brand of nationalism.

Debates Over Freedom of Expression and Pluralism: The rise of cultural nationalism has sparked intense debates over freedom of expression and the place of pluralism in Indian society.

Some artists, intellectuals, and journalists have voiced concerns over a perceived shrinking space for dissent and debate, citing instances of censorship and retaliation against those who criticize the government's policies. These debates underscore the tension between promoting a unified national identity and preserving the diverse voices that have traditionally characterized the Indian polity.

Community Initiatives and Resistance: In response to the challenges posed by the rise of cultural nationalism, various community groups and civil society organizations have initiated efforts to celebrate India's pluralistic heritage and promote inclusivity.

These initiatives aim to counteract the divisive aspects of cultural nationalism by fostering dialogue and understanding among different religious and cultural groups.

This detailed exploration of the societal impact highlights the polarized reactions to Modi's cultural nationalism, reflecting the broader challenges and debates it has sparked within India's pluralistic society. The section provides insight into the immediate effects of these policies and sets the stage for discussing the longer-term implications for unity, diversity, and the very fabric of Indian democracy.

Continuing with the detailed exploration of "Redefining National Identity" under Narendra Modi's leadership, the next focus is Celebrating Diversity. This section aims to highlight how, amidst the surge of cultural nationalism, there have been concerted efforts and programs to celebrate India's rich and diverse cultural heritage. These initiatives testify to the enduring strength of India's pluralistic values, even in times of heightened cultural nationalism.

Celebrating Diversity Detail

India's diversity is not just a fact of life but the soul of its national identity. Recognizing this, various government and non-governmental initiatives have sought to celebrate this diversity, highlighting the country's cultural, linguistic, and religious traditions. This section delves into specific programs and events to honor and preserve India's pluralistic fabric.

Festivals and Traditional Arts: The government has promoted national and regional festivals that showcase India's multicultural heritage, supporting events that highlight the traditions of minority communities alongside those of the Hindu majority. These festivals, often featuring traditional music, dance, and crafts, serve as platforms for cultural exchange and mutual appreciation among India's diverse communities.

Language Preservation and Promotion: Acknowledging the importance of India's linguistic diversity, efforts have been made to preserve and promote lesser-known languages and dialects. This includes establishing centers for classical languages and including multiple regional languages in educational curricula, aiming to foster a sense of pride and identity among speakers of these languages.

Heritage Conservation Projects: Projects aimed at conserving and revitalizing India's historical and cultural sites have also played a significant role in celebrating diversity. These initiatives, which cover a range of religious and cultural landmarks, underscore the government's commitment to preserving the physical manifestations of India's diverse heritage.

Inclusive Cultural Policies: While there has been a notable emphasis on Hindu cultural heritage, policies have also been formulated to ensure the representation and promotion of minority cultures. These include financial support for cultural institutions, scholarships for artists from various backgrounds, and international exchange programs that showcase India's diversity on the global stage.

Through these initiatives, the chapter illustrates the multifaceted efforts to celebrate and reinforce India's diversity amidst the challenges posed by the rise of cultural nationalism. By highlighting these examples, the narrative underscores the ongoing dialogue between the forces of cultural nationalism and the enduring values of pluralism and inclusivity that have characterized India's societal fabric.

Criticism from Secularists and Minorities Detail

This section delves into the criticisms and concerns of secular activists, minority communities, and political opponents regarding the rise of cultural nationalism under Narendra Modi's leadership.

These critiques are pivotal in understanding the broader implications of redefining national identity in a country as diverse as India.

Secular Activists' Concerns: Secular activists have been vocal about their apprehensions, arguing that the emphasis on Hindu cultural nationalism threatens to erode India's secular fabric. They contend that such an emphasis shifts the nation's foundational ethos from a pluralistic and inclusive identity towards a more homogenized and exclusionary one. Critics point to changes in educational curricula, the glorification of Hindu historical narratives, and the marginalization of secular and liberal voices as evidence of this shift. The fear is that this redefinition of identity could fundamentally alter the secular character of the Indian state envisioned by its founding fathers.

Minority Groups' Reactions: Minority communities, particularly Muslims and Christians, have expressed concern over their place in Modi's vision of India. Incidents of communal violence, beef bans, and the abrogation of Article 370 in Jammu and Kashmir are cited as actions that have heightened feelings of vulnerability among these communities. Critics argue that such policies and the rhetoric surrounding them contribute to a sense of alienation and second-class citizenship among minorities, undermining the principles of equality and fraternity enshrined in the Constitution.

Political Opposition: The political opposition has leveraged these concerns, accusing the Modi government of undermining India's democratic and secular principles in favor of a majoritarian agenda. Debates in the parliament and public forums often center on the balance between celebrating Hindu heritage and maintaining a commitment to secularism and minority rights. The opposition calls for a recommitment to the inclusive vision of India, emphasizing unity in diversity.

Intellectual and Cultural Debates: The rise of cultural nationalism has also sparked intellectual debates on the nature of Indian identity, the role of religion in public life, and the implications for democracy and social harmony. Academics, writers, and public intellectuals have contributed to a vibrant discourse, questioning the long-term effects of prioritizing one cultural narrative over others.

This detailed exploration of criticisms and debates surrounding cultural nationalism provides a nuanced view of the tensions and challenges facing India's pluralistic society. By presenting these perspectives, the chapter offers a comprehensive understanding of the diverse viewpoints and concerns that animate discussions on national identity in contemporary India.

Government's Stance on Diversity Detail

In the face of criticism and concerns regarding the rise of cultural nationalism, the government under Narendra Modi has articulated its stance on diversity and pluralism. This section examines the government's responses, policies, and initiatives aimed at reassuring minority communities and upholding India's pluralistic values amidst the push for a unified cultural identity.

Reassuring Minorities: The government has made several statements to reassure India's minority communities of their place and protection within the national fabric. Modi has often spoken of his commitment to "Sabka Saath, Sabka Vikas" (Together with all, Development for all), emphasizing an inclusive approach to governance. These assurances are evidence of the government's dedication to safeguarding the rights and well-being of all citizens, regardless of their religious or cultural background.

Legislative and Policy Measures: The chapter details various legislative and policy measures undertaken to promote social harmony and protect minority rights. These include programs aimed at economic upliftment, educational opportunities, and the protection of religious freedoms. The government's efforts to enhance minority representation in public institutions and improve access to government services are highlighted as part of its commitment to diversity and inclusivity.

Dialogue and Reconciliation Efforts: The government's initiatives to foster dialogue and reconciliation between community groups are examined. This includes the organization of interfaith dialogues, community engagement programs, and the promotion of cultural exchange events designed to bridge divides and build mutual understanding among India's diverse populations.

Critiques and Counterpoints: While detailing the government's stance, the section also acknowledges the critiques and counterpoints raised by skeptics who question the effectiveness and sincerity of these measures. The challenges in reconciling the promotion of a dominant cultural narrative with the protection of pluralistic values are discussed, providing a balanced view of the government's efforts and the ongoing societal debates.

This detailed account of the government's stance on diversity illuminates the complexities in navigating India's pluralistic landscape amidst the push for cultural nationalism. By presenting both the government's initiatives and the criticisms thereof, the chapter aims to offer a comprehensive perspective on the efforts to reconcile differences and maintain social harmony in contemporary India.

Conclusion Detail

As we conclude the chapter on "Redefining National Identity" within the broader context of Cultural and Societal Evolution under Narendra Modi's leadership, it's imperative to reflect on the nuanced interplay between cultural nationalism and India's pluralistic society. This section synthesizes insights from the detailed exploration of policies, societal impacts, celebrations of diversity, criticisms, and the government's stance to offer a forward-looking perspective on the evolution of India's national identity and the legacy of Modi's tenure.

Evolving National Identity: The chapter underscores that India's national identity is in flux, influenced by the resurgence of cultural nationalism. This evolution is marked by a heightened emphasis on Hindu cultural heritage, which has sparked pride and controversy.

The narrative of India as a Hindu nation, while resonating with many, has raised alarms about the potential marginalization of minority communities and the erosion of secular values. However, the chapter also highlights instances where diversity is celebrated and pluralism is championed, showcasing the enduring complexity of India's identity.

Future Trajectory: The chapter speculates on the future trajectory of national identity in India. It discusses the challenges and opportunities in balancing cultural nationalism with the need to maintain a cohesive, inclusive society. The potential for fostering a shared sense of identity that embraces diversity while celebrating a common heritage is explored. The chapter suggests that the key to India's unity and strength lies in its ability to honor its pluralistic values while navigating the waters of a dominant cultural narrative.

Legacy of Modi's Tenure: The chapter concludes with an assessment of Narendra Modi's potential legacy in terms of national identity.

It posits that Modi's tenure will be viewed through the lens of how successfully his government enhanced national pride without compromising the foundational principles of democracy and secularism. The impact of his policies and rhetoric on India's societal fabric, the integration of minority communities, and the global perception of India as a diverse yet unified nation are considered critical elements of this legacy.

By providing a balanced and insightful analysis, this chapter aims to give readers a deeper understanding of the complexities of redefining national identity in modern India. It encourages reflection on the delicate balance between fostering cultural pride and ensuring the inclusive, pluralistic ethos that has long defined the nation.

Reflecting on the journey through this chapter, we've navigated the intricate landscape of cultural nationalism and its implications for India's national identity. This exploration has not only shed light on the current dynamics but also set the stage for ongoing discussions about the future of India's diverse society.

CHAPTER 11

THE MEDIA LANDSCAPE

*"In the age of information,
media's role is not just to inform but to empower citizens,
serving as the bridge between government and the governed."*

— Narendra Modi

Analyzing changes in media engagement and press freedom, this chapter delves into the evolving dynamics of India's media landscape under Modi's governance, highlighting the challenges and opportunities in the digital age.

Introduction

In the evolving landscape of Indian politics and society, the role of media has undergone significant transformations, particularly under the leadership of Prime Minister Narendra Modi. Since assuming office in 2014, Modi has redefined the interface between the government and its citizens, leveraging traditional and digital media platforms to communicate, engage, and influence. This chapter, nestled within the broader narrative of Cultural and Societal Evolution in Part III, embarks on a critical yet balanced exploration of these transformations.

It delves into the nuances of media engagement, the dynamics of press freedom, and digital media's pivotal role in shaping public discourse in contemporary India.

Under Modi's governance, India has witnessed a paradigm shift in the media landscape, marked by innovative strategies and a significant emphasis on digital media. These changes reflect a broader global trend towards digitization but are uniquely tailored to the Indian context, resonating with the country's diverse and vast populace. The chapter aims to unpack these developments, offering insights into how strategic communication has been employed to bolster the government's image and counter dissent. It examines the intricate dance between maintaining a robust democratic discourse and the allegations of media manipulation and censorship that have surfaced.

The narrative arc of this exploration is structured to provide a holistic view, beginning with a historical overview that outlines the media's traditional role in Indian democracy. This backdrop is crucial for appreciating the magnitude of change under Modi's tenure. The subsequent sections delve into the rise of social media as a dominant force in political communication, the government's initiatives to enhance digital media presence, and the strategic media engagement tactics that Modi and his administration employ.

As the chapter progresses, it critically assesses allegations of censorship and the challenges the press faces in navigating the legal and political landscape. The enduring role of media as a watchdog and the challenges to press freedom under Modi's government are examined in depth, alongside the issue of digital disinformation and fake news—a global concern that has significant implications in the Indian context.

The conclusion reflects on the dual-edged nature of the media landscape's evolution under Modi, contemplating the balance between innovative engagement and concerns over press freedom.

The chapter speculates on future trends and the potential impact of emerging technologies on media and information dissemination in India. Through this exploration, readers are invited to consider the critical role of media in shaping not just public discourse but the very fabric of democracy and societal consciousness in the Modi era.

Historical Overview

Before the advent of Narendra Modi's tenure as Prime Minister in 2014, India's media landscape was deeply entrenched in the principles of democratic discourse, reflecting the nation's diverse, multilingual, and pluralistic society. The press played a crucial role in shaping public opinion, acting as a watchdog against power, and facilitating a vibrant public sphere for debate and discussion. Historically, Indian media evolved from the colonial-era press, which was instrumental in the independence movement, to a complex, multifaceted ecosystem comprising print, television, and, later, digital platforms.

The pre-Modi era was characterized by a relatively free press that vigorously reported and analyzed government actions, corruption, and social injustices. Despite challenges such as political pressure, ownership patterns affecting editorial independence, and legal hurdles like defamation laws, the media managed to maintain a significant degree of autonomy. Noteworthy is the period of the Emergency (1975-1977), when press freedom was severely curtailed, serving as a stark reminder of the importance of a free press in a democratic society. This historical context sets the stage for understanding the shifts and continuities in media engagement and press freedom under Modi's governance.

Transition to Modi's Era

With Narendra Modi's election in 2014, the media landscape witnessed transformative changes. Modi, a charismatic leader with a strong mandate, brought an innovative approach to media engagement.

Recognizing the power of media in shaping narratives and public perception, his administration leveraged both traditional and emerging digital platforms to unprecedented extents. This period saw a strategic shift towards more direct forms of communication, utilizing social media, mobile applications, and other digital platforms to bypass traditional media filters and directly reach the electorate.

The rise of digital media under Modi is not just a reflection of technological advancement but a deliberate and strategic choice. The government's initiatives, such as the Digital India campaign, aimed at increasing digital literacy and access, further facilitated this shift. This digital push was paralleled by a noticeable change in the relationship between the government and traditional media, with increasing concerns over press freedom, allegations of censorship, and the use of defamation laws to silence critics.

This historical overview underscores the significant shifts in India's media landscape, setting a comprehensive background for analyzing the intricate dynamics of media engagement, press freedom, and the role of digital media in the Modi era. It highlights the continuity of media's role in democratic discourse while pointing to new challenges and opportunities that have emerged with digital technology and strategic communication.

Expansion of Digital Media

The expansion of digital media under Prime Minister Narendra Modi represents a cornerstone of the transformation observed in the Indian media landscape. This shift has influenced political communication and has had profound implications for broader societal engagement with media. Central to this transformation is the rise of social media and significant government initiatives to boost India's digital infrastructure.

Rise of Social Media

Under Modi's leadership, social media platforms such as Twitter, Facebook, and Instagram have become pivotal in political communication and campaigning. Modi has been at the forefront of adopting social media, becoming one of the most followed world leaders on these platforms. This direct line of communication has enabled the Prime Minister and the Bharatiya Janata Party (BJP) to craft and disseminate their message without the traditional media gatekeeping, allowing for a more controlled and targeted outreach.

The strategic use of social media has been instrumental in mobilizing support, engaging with the youth, and shaping public opinion on key policy initiatives. The 2014 and 2019 general elections are prime examples of how social media campaigns, characterized by catchy hashtags, viral videos, and interactive posts, have significantly influenced electoral outcomes. These campaigns demonstrated the power of digital platforms in reaching out to India's vast and diverse population, many of whom are accessing the internet for the first time.

Government Initiatives

Parallel to the rise of social media, the Modi government launched several initiatives to enhance the country's digital infrastructure, facilitating greater media consumption and engagement.

The Digital India campaign, launched in 2015, stands out as a flagship program to transform India into a digitally empowered society and knowledge economy. This initiative focuses on three core components: developing a secure and stable digital infrastructure, the delivery of government services digitally, and universal digital literacy.

The Digital India campaign has had significant implications for media consumption, contributing to a surge in digital content creation, consumption, and dissemination.

It has also played a crucial role in democratizing access to information, breaking down traditional barriers to media access, and enabling citizens from remote and rural areas to participate in the digital revolution. This democratization of media access aligns with the government's broader vision of leveraging technology to foster development, governance, and social inclusion.

The expansion of digital media under Modi's governance has fundamentally altered the dynamics of media engagement in India. It has introduced new political communication paradigms, transformed how citizens interact with media and raised important questions about digital literacy, privacy, and the digital divide. As we delve deeper into the intricacies of media engagement strategies and the challenges to press freedom, it becomes evident that the digital revolution in India's media landscape is empowering and complex, offering new engagement opportunities while presenting new challenges for democracy and societal discourse.

Media Engagement Strategies

The Modi administration has pioneered innovative media engagement strategies that significantly diverge from traditional approaches. These strategies emphasize direct communication with the public, leveraging digital platforms and orchestrating public relations campaigns to shape public perception and promote government policies.

Direct Communication

A hallmark of Modi's media strategy has been the emphasis on direct communication channels, epitomized by the "Mann Ki Baat" radio program.

Launched in October 2014, this monthly radio address allows the Prime Minister to speak directly to the nation, discussing various topics, from government initiatives to social and cultural issues.

The program's simplicity, coupled with its reach to millions of Indians across urban and rural divides, exemplifies Modi's approach to bypassing traditional media outlets and establishing a personal connection with the citizenry. The use of social media and the NaMo App further reinforces this strategy, providing platforms for direct engagement without the intermediary role of the press. These channels have been used effectively to solicit policy feedback, announce new initiatives, and mobilize public support, leading to a more interactive and participatory form of political communication.

Public Relations Campaigns

Complementing direct communication, the Modi government has also deployed extensive public relations campaigns highlighting its achievements and policies. Campaigns such as "Swachh Bharat" (Clean India), "Make in India," and "Digital India" have been promoted aggressively across media platforms, utilizing a mix of traditional advertising, social media buzz, and public events. These campaigns are designed to inform and engage the public and create a narrative of progress and proactive governance. The use of celebrity endorsements, catchy slogans, and visually appealing content has been characteristic of these campaigns, aiming to capture the public's imagination and foster a sense of national pride. This approach reflects an understanding of the media as a powerful tool for nation-building and public diplomacy, leveraging the convergence of media platforms to maximize reach and impact.

Evaluation

The media engagement strategies employed by the Modi administration have undoubtedly transformed the landscape of political communication in India, offering lessons in the power of direct communication and strategic public relations.

However, these strategies also raise important questions about the balance between persuasion and propaganda, the potential for bypassing critical media scrutiny, and the implications for democratic discourse. As the media landscape continues to evolve, the effectiveness and impact of these strategies will be subject to ongoing debate and analysis. What remains clear is that the Modi era has marked a significant shift in the dynamics of media engagement, reflecting broader global trends toward digitalization and personalized political communication.

Press Freedom and Criticism

The transformation of the media landscape under Prime Minister Narendra Modi's governance has raised significant concerns regarding press freedom in India. While the expansion of digital media and direct communication strategies have democratized information dissemination, allegations of media censorship, intimidation, and the use of legal mechanisms to silence critics have cast a shadow over these developments.

Allegations of Censorship

Critics argue that there has been a concerted effort to control the narrative surrounding the government's policies and actions. Instances of media outlets facing financial audits, regulatory scrutiny, or direct political pressure following critical reporting have been reported. Moreover, the rise of digital media, while offering new platforms for expression, has facilitated a more surveilled and controlled media environment where dissenting voices can be more easily targeted and suppressed. Journalists and media organizations that have been vocal in their critique of the government often find themselves at the receiving end of online harassment campaigns, legal challenges, and, in some cases, physical threats. These tactics endanger journalists' safety and instill a culture of self-censorship within the media industry, undermining the democratic role of the press as a watchdog.

Defamation and Legal Challenges

The legal environment in India has posed additional challenges to press freedom. The use of defamation laws, both civil and criminal, has been a particular concern. Critics claim the government and its supporters often leverage these laws to intimidate journalists and media outlets, discouraging them from pursuing investigative reporting or critical analysis of government policies. The Supreme Court of India's stance on defamation laws has been intensely debated.

While the court has upheld the constitutionality of criminal defamation, it has also recognized the need to balance such laws with the fundamental right to freedom of speech and expression. The application of these laws, however, continues to be a contentious issue, with media advocates calling for reforms to protect journalists and ensure the free flow of information.

Role of Media in Democracy

Despite these challenges, the media in India continues to play a critical role in democratic governance. Instances of investigative journalism leading to public revelations and accountability, such as uncovering corruption scandals or highlighting social injustices, underscore the importance of a free and vibrant press. The debate over press freedom in the Modi era reflects broader tensions between the government's media engagement strategies and the foundational principles of democratic discourse.

The challenges to press freedom under Modi's governance highlight the delicate balance between government-media relations and the need for a robust, independent press in a democracy. As India continues to navigate the complexities of the digital age, protecting press freedom remains a pivotal issue, central to the health of its democratic institutions and the rights of its citizens.

Digital Disinformation and Fake News

In the contemporary media landscape, the proliferation of digital disinformation and fake news presents a formidable challenge in India and globally.

Under Prime Minister Narendra Modi's tenure, the issue has gained particular prominence due to the widespread use of social media and digital platforms for political communication. This section explores the challenges digital disinformation poses and the efforts to combat it, alongside the nuanced role of government and media collaboration in addressing this issue.

Combatting Misinformation

The Indian government, recognizing the potential of misinformation to disrupt social harmony and influence electoral processes, has taken steps to mitigate the spread of fake news. Initiatives include establishing fact-checking units within governmental bodies and collaborations with social media platforms to identify and remove false information. For example, the Press Information Bureau (PIB) has actively debunked false news about government policies and public health issues, especially during the COVID-19 pandemic.

However, the battle against misinformation is fraught with challenges. The sheer volume of content, the speed of dissemination, and the anonymity afforded by digital platforms make it difficult to control the spread of false information effectively. Moreover, the blurred lines between misinformation, free speech, and political propaganda complicate the issue. Efforts to curb fake news have been criticized when perceived as overreaching or as attempts to suppress dissenting voices under the guise of combating misinformation.

Government and Media Collaboration

Instances of collaboration between the government and media organizations in spreading information or countering misinformation highlight the potential for positive synergies in addressing the challenges of the digital age. Such collaborations have ranged from public awareness campaigns to partnerships with technology companies to develop tools and algorithms to flag fake news.

However, this collaboration raises questions about media independence and the potential for governmental influence over media content.

The balance between cooperative efforts to ensure the accuracy of information and safeguarding the autonomy of the press is delicate and subject to ongoing debate.

Assessment

The issue of digital disinformation and fake news in the Modi era illustrates the complex interplay between technological advancements, political communication, and democratic values. While efforts to combat misinformation are crucial for maintaining public trust and social stability, they must be balanced with commitments to freedom of expression and media independence. The rise of fake news underscores the public's need for media literacy and critical thinking skills, highlighting an area where the government and media organizations can play a constructive role.

As India grapples with the challenges of misinformation in the digital age, the strategies adopted by the Modi government and the media's response will have significant implications for democracy and public discourse. The fight against fake news, thus, is not just a technical challenge but a democratic imperative, requiring a nuanced and collaborative approach that respects both the need for accurate information and the principles of a free society.

Conclusion and Future Trends

As we reflect upon "The Media Landscape" under Prime Minister Narendra Modi's leadership, it becomes clear that the intersection of media, technology, and politics has undergone profound transformations. These changes, marked by the rise of digital platforms, innovative engagement strategies, and challenges to press freedom, offer a nuanced vista into the evolving dynamics of media engagement and its implications for democratic discourse in India.

Assessing the Media Landscape

The Modi era has been characterized by a strategic embrace of digital media to foster direct communication with the populace, circumventing traditional media's gatekeeping role.

Initiatives like the Digital India campaign and Modi's personal use of social media have reshaped political communication, making it more immediate, interactive, and far-reaching. However, alongside these advancements, concerns regarding press freedom, allegations of censorship, and the complexities of combating digital disinformation have emerged as critical issues.

The balance between harnessing digital media for governance and ensuring a free, independent press remains a delicate endeavor. While the government's media engagement strategies have undeniably broadened the scope and reach of political communication, they have also sparked debates about the implications for democratic engagement and the health of the public sphere.

Future of Media in India

The future of media in India appears poised at the crossroads of further technological innovation and the ongoing struggle to uphold democratic ideals.

Emerging technologies like artificial intelligence, machine learning, and blockchain hold the potential further to transform media production, distribution, and consumption. These advancements could enhance news personalization, improve fake news detection, and even redefine the nature of journalistic content. However, they also present new challenges for privacy, security, and ethical considerations.

The role of media in shaping public discourse and democracy will continue to evolve, reflecting broader social, technological, and political trends. The critical question remains:

How will these transformations impact the core values of press freedom, accountability, and the right to information?

As India navigates these changes, the need for vigilant, independent journalism and informed, critical engagement by the public has never been more crucial.

The Role of Media in Shaping Public Discourse

In conclusion, the media landscape in the Modi era offers a compelling case study of the power of media in shaping public discourse, democracy, and the collective consciousness of a nation.

As India looks to the future, the media's role as a pillar of democracy and a forum for public debate will continue to be central. Balancing the innovative use of digital platforms with the imperative to protect press freedom and combat misinformation will be key to ensuring that the media remains a vibrant and democratic space for all Indians.

The media journey in the Modi era encapsulates the challenges and opportunities of our times, serving as a mirror to the broader global conversation about the role of media in society.

As we move forward, the lessons learned and the questions raised during this period will undoubtedly inform the ongoing dialogue about democracy, technology, and the indispensable role of the media in shaping the world we live in.

This detailed exploration of "The Media Landscape" under Narendra Modi's governance has aimed to provide a comprehensive analysis of the complex interplay between government and media, offering insights into the evolving dynamics of media engagement, the challenges to press freedom, and the critical role of media in sustaining democratic discourse in the Modi era.

PART IV: CHALLENGES AND CRITIQUES

"Criticism is the bedrock of democracy.
It makes a democracy strong and resilient."
— Narendra Modi

CHAPTER 12

THE CONTOURS OF CRITICISM

"In the fabric of democracy,
criticism is not a stain but a strain that strengthens it,
encouraging dialogue and development."

— Narendra Modi

This chapter embarks on a balanced exploration of the criticisms faced by Narendra Modi's administration. It delves into the policy backlashes, governance challenges, and the debates surrounding the implications of his reforms on India's democratic fabric and secular ethos. Through a nuanced discussion, this section aims to shed light on the complexities and controversies that accompany significant change.

Introduction

In the annals of India's democratic journey, the tenure of Prime Minister Narendra Modi stands out for its ambitious vision and the polarized reactions it has elicited. Ascending to power in 2014, Modi's administration was ushered in on a wave of high expectations, buoyed by promises of sweeping economic reforms, good governance, and social upliftment. However, inherent in the fabric of democracy is the principle that no administration is immune to criticism.

This chapter, "The Contours of Criticism," aims to navigate the intricate landscape of critiques Modi's government faced, traversing economic policy, social and cultural initiatives, environmental stewardship, governance, and institutional integrity.

The scope of criticism is as broad as it is complex, touching upon various facets of governance and policy implementation. Acknowledging the significant support that Modi's government has garnered, it is also essential to explore the voices of dissent and critique, for they play a crucial role in the democratic process. This exploration is conducted with a commitment to balance, seeking to offer an informative and comprehensive overview of the criticisms while maintaining an educational tone and a respectful approach. Through this lens, we aim to understand the criticisms themselves and the thematic elements of accountability and governance that they underscore.

Demonetization Fallout

In a dramatic televised address on the evening of November 8, 2016, Prime Minister Narendra Modi announced the immediate withdrawal of ₹500 and ₹1000 banknotes from circulation, a move that rendered 86% of India's currency invalid overnight. This unprecedented step, termed "demonetization," was presented as a bold strike against black money, corruption, counterfeit currency, and terrorism financing. However, the fallout of this decision quickly became a focal point of intense criticism and debate across the nation and beyond.

Impact on the Economy

The rationale behind demonetization was to cleanse the system of illicit wealth and promote a cashless economy. However, the immediate aftermath saw a significant disruption in the informal sector, which accounts for a substantial portion of India's economy and employment. Small businesses, agriculture, and the daily wage sector, predominantly cash-reliant, faced severe hardships.

A liquidity crunch ensued, with long queues at banks and ATMs becoming common as people scrambled to exchange their old currency notes.

The GDP growth rate showed a noticeable decline in the quarters following demonetization. Critics argue that the move dented economic momentum, with the informal sector bearing the brunt of the impact. The lack of adequate preparation and sudden announcement were major policy implementation flaws.

Public Hardship

The immediate consequence of demonetization was widespread public hardship. Reports of savings being wiped out, difficulties in accessing medical services due to cash shortages, and disruptions to daily life painted a grim picture. The move was criticized for lacking empathy towards the commoner, especially in rural areas with sparse banking infrastructure.

While the government pushed for digital payments as an alternative, the transition was far from seamless, highlighting the digital divide in the country.

The move was seen as well-intentioned but poorly executed, with the planning and rollout phases criticized for not considering the full spectrum of Indian economic and social life.

Analysis and Critique

Economists and analysts have debated the long-term impacts of demonetization, with opinions divided on its success or failure. While some point to an increase in digital transactions and a widening of the tax base as positive outcomes, others highlight the job losses, economic slowdown, and the pain inflicted on the most vulnerable sections of society as evidence of its failure.

The narrative arc detailing the response to and outcomes of these criticisms reflects a complex interplay of policy intentions, execution challenges, and the resilience of the Indian public. The government defended the move as a necessary pain for long-term gain, citing increased tax compliance and a crackdown on illicit financial activities. However, the critiques emphasize the need for a more nuanced approach to policymaking, one that thoroughly considers the socio-economic realities of India's diverse populace.

GST Implementation Concerns

The Goods and Services Tax (GST), introduced on July 1, 2017, was heralded as a transformative step towards simplifying India's complex tax structure, unifying the country into a single market by replacing many state and central taxes with a single tax. While the intent behind the GST was to streamline tax administration, eliminate tax-on-tax (cascading effect), and increase compliance, its implementation has been fraught with challenges and criticisms.

Complexity and Compliance Burdens

One of the primary criticisms of the GST rollout was its complexity. The new tax regime introduced multiple tax slabs (0%, 5%, 12%, 18%, and 28%), causing confusion among businesses, especially small and medium-sized enterprises (SMEs). The requirement for businesses to file monthly returns was seen as a significant compliance burden, adding to the operational costs of running a business.

Though innovative, the digital infrastructure for GST filing faced teething issues, with many businesses struggling to navigate the GST portal due to technical glitches and the complexity of the filing process.

Impact on Small Businesses

Small businesses, which form the backbone of the Indian economy, were particularly hard hit by the GST's implementation challenges.

Many SMEs lacked the resources to adapt quickly to the new system, resulting in disruptions to their operations. The compliance costs and the necessity to upgrade or install new IT systems for GST filing posed significant financial strains on small businesses, some already operating on thin margins.

The transitional economic slowdown following the GST's introduction was another point of criticism. While the long-term benefits of GST for the economy were widely acknowledged, the immediate aftermath saw a contraction in some sectors, adding to the economic pressures stemming from the demonetization move a year earlier. Critics argued that more could have been done to ease the transition for small businesses and to prepare the economy for such a major overhaul.

Economic Transition and Adjustments

The transitional slowdown in the economy post-GST rollout was attributed to adjustments in the supply chain and inventory management as businesses adapted to the new tax regime. While the government took steps to ease the transition, including revising tax rates and simplifying filing procedures over time, critics argue that the initial implementation phase could have been managed more effectively to minimize disruption.

The government's response to these criticisms was multifaceted. Efforts were made to streamline the GST filing process, including introducing a simplified return filing system and reducing tax rates for certain goods and services to alleviate the burden on consumers and businesses. These adjustments reflect the government's willingness to respond to feedback and fine-tune policies to the economy's practical challenges.

Responses and Public Discourse

The discourse around the GST implementation highlights a crucial aspect of policymaking in a democracy: the need for ongoing dialogue between the government, businesses, and the public.

The criticisms and challenges faced by the GST rollout have spurred debates on the effectiveness of policy implementation and the importance of readiness and support mechanisms for such significant economic reforms.

Government officials and policymakers have defended the GST as a necessary step towards a more efficient and transparent tax system. They point to the gradual increase in GST collections and the number of new businesses registering under GST as indicators of its success. Moreover, moving towards a digital tax system is seen as a leap forward in combating tax evasion and increasing compliance.

Conclusion

While ambitious and fraught with initial challenges, the GST implementation represents a significant step in India's economic reform journey. The criticisms it faced underscore the complexities of overhauling a tax system in a diverse and vast economy like India's. These critiques and the government's responses to them illustrate the dynamic nature of policy implementation, where adjustments and improvements are necessary to align with the ground realities.

Through a detailed exploration of these challenges and the measures taken to address them, the chapter "The Contours of Criticism" aims to provide readers with a nuanced understanding of the intricacies of implementing large-scale economic reforms.

The narrative arc, from the unveiling of the GST to the ongoing adjustments and dialogue, reflects the essential role of critique and feedback in the democratic process, highlighting the importance of adaptability and responsiveness in governance.

Citizenship Amendment Act and NRC

The Citizenship Amendment Act (CAA), passed in December 2019, amended the Indian Citizenship Act of 1955 to provide a pathway for non-Muslim immigrants from Afghanistan, Bangladesh, and Pakistan who entered India on or before December 31, 2014, to obtain Indian citizenship. The Act sparked widespread controversy and criticism, with detractors arguing that it undermines India's secular constitution by making religion a basis for citizenship.

Undermining Secular Principles

Critics argue that the CAA, by explicitly excluding Muslims, deviates from India's foundational secular principles, which mandate equal treatment under the law irrespective of religion. This exclusion raised fears among India's Muslim community and secular activists about the marginalization of Muslims and the erosion of secularism as a core democratic value.

Social Unrest and Protests

Introducing the CAA led to nationwide protests, with millions taking to the streets in opposition. The protests were marked by a broad coalition of participants, including students, activists, and Muslim community members. Critics of the CAA were joined by those concerned about the National Register of Citizens (NRC), a proposed exercise aimed at identifying illegal immigrants, which had already been implemented in Assam. Together, the CAA and NRC fueled apprehensions of statelessness for millions, particularly among Muslims, and the prospect of detention centers for those unable to prove their citizenship.

The government's response to the protests has been another point of criticism, with allegations of excessive force used against demonstrators and attempts to quell dissent through arrests and internet shutdowns. This handling of social unrest has raised concerns about the state of democracy and freedom of expression in India.

Responses and Public Discourse

The government defends the CAA by stating its intent to protect persecuted minorities from neighboring countries and denies any discriminatory intent against Muslims.

It also argues that the NRC is necessary to identify illegal immigrants, irrespective of their religion. However, the lack of clarity on how the NRC would be implemented nationally, combined with the CAA, has contributed to widespread fear and uncertainty.

The controversy surrounding the CAA and NRC has sparked a vibrant public discourse on citizenship, national identity, and secularism in India. The role of media, civil society, and opposition parties has been pivotal in shaping the debate, highlighting the deep divisions and democratic engagement within the country.

Conclusion

The criticisms of the CAA and the proposed NRC underscore the tension between national security, citizenship, and India's secular constitution. This chapter's exploration of the "Contours of Criticism" reveals the complexities of governing a diverse and democratic society. The narrative arc, from the legislation's introduction to the societal response and the government's defense, reflects the dynamic interplay between policy-making and public expectation, emphasizing the critical role of critique in a democracy.

The ongoing debates and protests against the CAA and NRC highlight concerns about the policies themselves and broader issues of governance, secularism, and the rights of minorities. These developments offer valuable insights into the challenges of balancing national security concerns with the principles of equality and secularism, underscoring the importance of dialogue, transparency, and inclusivity in policy formulation and implementation.

Centralization of Power

The Narendra Modi administration has been frequently critiqued for the perceived centralization of power within the Prime Minister's Office (PMO), with implications that resonate through the corridors of India's federal structure and democratic institutions. It is argued that this centralization has a significant bearing on governance, federalism, and the autonomy of state governments.

Implications for Federalism

Critics argue that the centralization of decision-making power in the PMO undermines the principles of federalism, a foundational feature of India's constitutional framework. Federalism in India ensures a balance of power between the central government and the states, allowing for regional autonomy and accommodating India's vast diversity. However, concerns have been raised about state governments' diminishing role and influence in policy formulation and implementation, particularly in areas that directly impact their socio-economic landscapes.

Relationship with State Governments

The centralization narrative includes tensions between the central government and states, especially those governed by opposition parties. Critics point to instances where the central government is perceived to have bypassed or overruled state governments on matters within their purview, leading to allegations of eroding the cooperative spirit essential for India's federal structure. This tension is particularly evident in financial relations, with states expressing concerns over the distribution of resources and fiscal autonomy in the wake of centralized policies like the GST.

Analysis and Critique

The critique of power centralization extends beyond federalism to encompass the broader implications for democratic governance.

It raises questions about the concentration of decision-making authority and its impact on the checks and balances inherent in a vibrant democracy.

The centralization of power limits the scope for dissenting voices and diverse viewpoints in the policymaking process, potentially leading to a governance model that prioritizes efficiency over democratic deliberation.

Responses and Public Discourse

In response, the government has often highlighted the need for strong leadership and decisive action to achieve national development goals and maintain national security. Proponents argue that a certain degree of centralization is necessary to streamline governance, cut through bureaucratic red tape, and implement policies effectively in a country as large and diverse as India.

The public discourse around centralization of power is deeply intertwined with broader debates on governance models, democracy, and development. The media, civil society, and academic institutions have played a crucial role in articulating the nuances of this critique, contributing to a lively debate on the future of India's democratic and federal structure.

Conclusion

The criticisms surrounding the centralization of power within the Modi administration offer a lens through which to examine the tensions between efficiency in governance and the principles of federalism and democracy. This chapter's exploration underscores the importance of maintaining a delicate balance between strong leadership and preserving democratic norms and institutions.

The ongoing dialogue between the government, opposition, civil society, and the public indicates the vibrant democratic ethos that characterizes India, highlighting the essential role of critique and dissent in shaping the nation's future.

Environmental Policy Criticisms

The Modi administration's environmental policies have been a point of contention, attracting criticism for prioritizing industrial and infrastructure development at the perceived expense of environmental conservation and the rights of local communities.

These criticisms are set against India's rapid economic growth and its implications for sustainable development.

Development vs. Conservation

Critics argue that the government's push for large-scale infrastructure projects, such as highways, railways, and industrial corridors, often overlooks the environmental degradation and ecological balance. Projects like the Central Vista redevelopment in New Delhi and the new coal mining initiatives have sparked debates about the cost of development in terms of environmental sustainability. Environmental impact assessments (EIAs) have been a particular focus of criticism concerning their rigor and transparency and the ease with which environmental clearances are granted for big projects.

Impact on Ecosystems and Local Communities

The impact of development projects on local ecosystems and communities is another significant area of critique. Large infrastructure projects in ecologically sensitive areas, such as the Northeast and the Western Ghats, have raised alarms over biodiversity loss, deforestation, and the displacement of indigenous populations. Critics highlight the need for a more balanced approach considering environmental sustainability and economic development.

The government's amendments to environmental regulations and proposed changes to the EIA notification have been met with public outcry and protests from environmental activists, who argue that these moves could dilute environmental safeguards and limit public participation in environmental governance.

Responses and Public Discourse

The government defends its environmental policies by emphasizing the need for sustainable development and highlighting initiatives to boost renewable energy, afforestation, and conservation efforts. It argues that development and environmental protection must go hand in hand to meet the aspirations of a growing economy and a large population.

The discourse around environmental policies in India is vibrant and multifaceted, involving activists, policymakers, industry stakeholders, and the general public. The debate underscores the complex challenge of balancing economic growth with environmental sustainability in a developing country like India.

Conclusion

The criticism of the Modi administration's environmental policies reflects broader concerns about the sustainability of India's development model. These critiques serve as a reminder of the importance of integrating environmental considerations into the heart of policymaking and the need for a holistic approach that does not compromise the planet's health for short-term gains.

This chapter's narrative arc of environmental policy criticism underscores the critical role of public engagement, transparency, and accountability in environmental governance. It highlights the ongoing dialogue between the government, civil society, and environmental stakeholders as essential to shaping environmentally sustainable policies and conducive to economic development.

This dialogue is a testament to the dynamic nature of democracy, where critique and dissent pave the way for more inclusive and sustainable policy frameworks.

This detailed exploration through the chapter "The Contours of Criticism" has provided a comprehensive overview of the challenges and critiques faced by the Narendra Modi administration, offering insights into the complex interplay between governance, policy-making, and democratic engagement. The analysis reflects the essential role of constructive criticism in a vibrant democracy, facilitating a deeper understanding of the dynamics between government actions and public expectations.

CHAPTER 13

DEMOCRACY AND SECULARISM DEBATED

*"Democracy and secularism are the cornerstones of our nation,
guiding us toward a future where
every voice is heard, and every belief respected."*

— Narendra Modi

Delving into concerns over democratic practices and secular values in contemporary India, this chapter examines the discourse surrounding the state of democracy and secularism. It critically assesses the impact of Modi's policies and leadership style on India's pluralistic society, exploring the juxtaposition of growth with governance and tradition with modernity.

Introduction

India's democratic fabric is woven with threads of diversity, pluralism, and a commitment to secularism, principles enshrined in its Constitution since 1950. As the world's largest democracy, India has navigated the complex interplay of maintaining democratic integrity while fostering a secular state that ensures religious freedom and equality before the law. This delicate balance is pivotal not only for India's internal harmony but also for its international image.

Foundational Principles of Democracy and Secularism in India

The Indian Constitution lays the groundwork for a democratic polity based on justice, liberty, equality, and fraternity principles. Secularism in India does not imply a separation of religion from the state but denotes the state's equal treatment of all religions. This nuanced approach to secularism accommodates India's immense religious diversity, ensuring that no single religion dominates the others.

The Heightened Debates Under Modi's Leadership

Since Narendra Modi assumed office in 2014, his tenure has been marked by significant achievements and controversies. One of the most contentious aspects has been the debate over the health of India's democracy and secular fabric.

Critics argue that under Modi's leadership, India has witnessed a centralization of power, challenges to freedom of expression, and a perceived erosion of secular values—issues that have sparked intense debate and concern both within India and internationally.

The introduction of policies perceived to favor the majority Hindu population, such as the Citizenship Amendment Act (CAA) and the abrogation of Article 370 in Jammu and Kashmir, have raised questions about the commitment to secularism and democratic norms. These actions and the government's stance on various civil liberties issues have led to widespread protests, debates, and discussions about the future direction of Indian democracy and secularism. This chapter aims to explore these debates in-depth, providing a balanced and thoughtful examination of the challenges to democracy and secularism in India under Modi's leadership. Through an analysis of electoral integrity, media freedom, civil society, dissent, challenges to secularism, and the state of judicial independence, we will seek to understand the complexities and nuances of these critical issues.

By setting the stage with a clear understanding of the foundational principles and the current debates, this chapter will offer readers a comprehensive view of the challenges, debates, and perspectives that define this pivotal moment in India's political and social evolution.

Detailed Analysis of Democratic Processes and Practices

The cornerstone of any democracy is its electoral process and the functioning of its legislative bodies. These areas have been the focus of significant scrutiny and debate in India in recent years.

Electoral Integrity

Concerns around Electronic Voting Machines (EVMs): Skepticism over the reliability and tamper-proof nature of EVMs has been a recurring theme among some political parties and civil society groups. Despite the Election Commission of India's assurances regarding the security features of EVMs, allegations of potential manipulation have surfaced in various elections since 2014.

Voter Suppression Allegations: There have been reports of voter disenfranchisement, where segments of the population, particularly in marginalized communities, have allegedly been excluded from electoral rolls. Such incidents raise questions about the inclusivity and fairness of the electoral process.

Role and Criticisms of the Election Commission: The Election Commission (EC), tasked with ensuring free and fair elections, has faced criticism for perceived partisanship and inadequacies in enforcing model code of conduct violations. The independence of the EC is crucial for maintaining electoral integrity, and any questions about its impartiality can undermine confidence in the electoral process.

Parliamentary Functioning

Passage of Bills without Adequate Debate: One of the major criticisms of the current administration has been the rapid passage of significant bills, sometimes within days of their introduction, without extensive debate or scrutiny. This practice has led to concerns about the erosion of parliamentary democracy and the quality of legislation being passed.

Use of Ordinances: The government's increasing reliance on ordinances to enact laws, bypassing the parliamentary process, has been another point of contention. Critics argue that this undermines the legislative scrutiny by Parliament and concentrates power within the executive branch.

Impact on Legislative Scrutiny: The reduced opportunity for debate and the tendency to pass bills without referring them to standing committees have raised concerns about the thoroughness of legislative scrutiny. This trend is seen as detrimental to the democratic process, limiting the ability of opposition parties and the wider parliamentary system to hold the government to account.

This analysis of democratic processes and practices highlights concerns regarding the integrity of elections and the functioning of Parliament in India. These issues form a critical part of the debate over the health of democracy under Narendra Modi's leadership, touching upon fundamental aspects of governance and political engagement in the country.

Examining these areas is essential for understanding the broader discussions on democracy and secularism in India, providing a foundation for exploring other related issues such as freedom of expression, civil liberties, and the challenges to secularism.

Exploration of Freedom of Expression and Civil Liberties

Media Freedom

Censorship and Government Pressure: Concerns have been raised about increasing censorship and self-censorship within the Indian media landscape. Reports of government pressure on media outlets, including financial pressures through advertising allocations and regulatory actions, have highlighted challenges to media freedom. Instances where journalists and media organizations face backlash for critical reporting, have underscored the precarious state of press freedom in India.

Impact on Journalistic Independence: The environment of pressure and potential repercussions for critical reporting have led to questions about the independence of the media. The rise of digital media platforms has provided alternative spaces for journalism, yet they, too, face challenges such as internet shutdowns and legal actions.

Civil Society and Dissent

Treatment of Activists and Critics: The space for civil society and dissent in India has been scrutinized, especially with the treatment of activists, NGOs, and government critics. Laws like the Unlawful Activities (Prevention) Act (UAPA) and sedition laws have been used against individuals and groups, raising concerns about the shrinking space for dissent and dialogue.

Laws Impacting Civil Liberties: The use of legal frameworks to curb dissent, including internet shutdowns, has been a significant issue. The government's stance on these measures, often justified on national security or public order grounds, has been a contention, with critics arguing they infringe on fundamental rights and civil liberties. This section has shed light on the significant challenges to freedom of expression and civil liberties in contemporary India.

By examining the state of media freedom and the constraints faced by civil society and activists, we gain insight into the broader debates around democracy and secularism under Narendra Modi's tenure. Exploring these themes is crucial for understanding the dynamics of political and social discourse in India, contributing to the overall analysis of democratic integrity, pluralism, and the health of the civil society framework.

Examination of Secularism and Communal Harmony

Challenges to Secularism

Policies Perceived as Favoring the Majority Community: There have been significant concerns regarding policies and actions that are perceived to favor the majority Hindu community. The Citizenship Amendment Act (CAA), which provides a pathway for non-Muslim immigrants from neighboring countries to gain Indian citizenship, has been particularly controversial, with critics arguing that it undermines India's secular principles.

Impact on Communal Harmony: Actions such as the abrogation of Article 370 in Jammu and Kashmir and the verdict on the Ayodhya dispute have sparked debates about their long-term impact on communal harmony. Critics contend such moves have exacerbated community tensions and challenged the nation's secular fabric.

Interfaith Relations

Communal Violence: Incidents of communal violence, such as the riots in Delhi in February 2020, have raised serious concerns about the state of interfaith relations in India. These events highlight the fragility of communal harmony and the need for effective measures to foster inter-community dialogue and reconciliation.

Debates over Religious Conversions: Allegations of "love jihad" and the passing of anti-conversion laws in several states have further polarized opinions. Some see these developments as attempts to regulate personal choices and infringe upon religious freedom, affecting the state's secular character. This analysis of secularism and communal harmony reveals deep-seated challenges and concerns within the Indian societal and political landscape. The balance between maintaining India's secular ethos and addressing communal tensions is critical for the nation's unity and democratic health. Exploring these issues provides a comprehensive understanding of the complexities surrounding secularism and communal harmony in contemporary India, reflecting on the broader implications for democracy, civil liberties, and the inclusive character of the nation under Narendra Modi's leadership.

Government and Judiciary Relations Analysis

Judicial Independence

Appointment Process of Judges: The collegium system for appointing judges to the higher judiciary has been a point of contention, with the government proposing changes that critics argue could undermine the independence of the judiciary. Debates around the National Judicial Appointments Commission (NJAC) and subsequent Supreme Court rulings reflect the ongoing struggle between the judiciary and the executive over control of judicial appointments.

Pressures on the Judiciary: There have been concerns about the executive's influence on the judiciary, including allegations of pressuring judges through investigations and surveillance.

Such actions, real or perceived, can have implications for the impartiality and independence of the judiciary, affecting public trust in the judicial system.

Legal Framework and Human Rights

Debates over Civil Liberties and Human Rights Protections: Recent years have seen significant legal and constitutional challenges, including the right to privacy judgment and internet shutdowns. The use of the Unlawful Activities (Prevention) Act (UAPA) and sedition laws to detain activists, journalists, and critics has sparked debates about the balance between national security and civil liberties.

Right to Protest and Internet Shutdowns: The government's response to protests, particularly the farmers' protests and the Citizenship Amendment Act (CAA) protests, including the use of internet shutdowns and legal actions against protestors, has raised questions about the commitment to democratic principles and the right to dissent.

This analysis of government and judiciary relations highlights the critical issues at the intersection of judicial independence, legal frameworks, and human rights in India. The balance between ensuring national security, upholding civil liberties, and maintaining an independent judiciary is central to the health of India's democracy and secularism.

By examining these aspects, the chapter sheds light on the challenges and debates surrounding the government's stance on democracy, secularism, and civil liberties, offering a nuanced perspective on the implications for the rule of law and democratic governance in contemporary India.

Responses to Critiques and Government's Stance

Government's Perspective

Upholding Democratic Processes: The Modi government has consistently argued that its policies and actions are aimed at strengthening India's democratic framework and ensuring the country's unity and integrity.

It has cited the electoral mandate as validating its approach and policies, emphasizing its commitment to the nation's development and security.

Measures for Secularism and Civil Liberties: In response to criticisms about affecting India's secular ethos, the government has reiterated its commitment to treating all citizens equally, regardless of religion. It has also defended using certain laws and actions, such as the Citizenship Amendment Act (CAA) and internet shutdowns, as necessary measures for national security and public order.

Public and International Reaction

Civil Society's Response: The government's stance and actions have prompted significant debate within India, with civil society organizations, activists, and a section of the media voicing concerns about the implications for democracy and secularism. Large-scale protests, like those against the CAA, have demonstrated the depth of public engagement and dissent.

International Community's Concerns: International human rights organizations and some foreign governments have expressed concerns about the state of human rights and democratic practices in India. Media freedom, treatment of activists, and religious freedom have been highlighted in various reports and statements, calling for adherence to international norms and standards.

Reflecting on Democracy and Secularism: Conclusion and Looking Ahead

In reflecting on the state of democracy and secularism in India, it is evident that Narendra Modi's tenure has been a period of intense debate and scrutiny. The challenges to democratic practices, secular values, and civil liberties under his leadership have sparked national and international discussions about the country's future direction.

The balance between governance, security, and preserving fundamental rights is a complex endeavor that requires continuous dialogue, engagement, and adjustments. Active citizenship, judicial oversight, and political engagement become paramount in addressing these debates and ensuring that India's democratic and secular credentials are maintained and strengthened.

Looking ahead, the future of democracy and secularism in India will likely continue to be shaped by the interplay between government policies, judicial interventions, and the active participation of civil society. The legacy of Modi's tenure, in terms of its impact on India's democratic and secular framework, will be a subject of analysis for years to come, with the hope that the foundational principles of democracy and secularism remain robust and vibrant.

This chapter has provided a comprehensive view of the critical issues, challenges, and debates surrounding democracy and secularism in contemporary India, offering insights into the complexities of governing a diverse and democratic society in the 21st century. The exploration of democracy and secularism under Narendra Modi's leadership concludes here. This detailed analysis has aimed to offer a nuanced understanding of the pivotal moments and debates that have defined this era in India's political and social evolution.

PART V:
PROJECTING THE FUTURE

"The 21st century is India's century.
It is the century of knowledge, and
India has always been a knowledge hub."
— Narendra Modi

CHAPTER 14

INDIA'S PLACE ON THE WORLD STAGE

"As India asserts its place on the world stage,
our goal is not just to contribute to our own development but to be
an active participant in shaping a global future that is bright for all."

— Narendra Modi

Investigating Modi's foreign policy achievements and aspirations for India's global standing, this chapter explores how India has navigated its international relations under his leadership. From strategic alliances to economic partnerships, the narrative highlights India's efforts to assert its influence while contributing to global peace and stability.

Introduction

Global Ambitions

Under Narendra Modi's leadership, India's global ambitions have been articulated through the vision of "Atmanirbhar Bharat" or self-reliant India. This vision emphasizes India's economic independence and its assertive global stance.

Modi envisions India as a pivotal player in international affairs, advocating for a multipolar world where India is one of the leading voices. This ambition is reflected in India's proactive approach to forming strategic partnerships, engaging in global governance, and asserting its influence in international conflict resolution and climate change negotiations.

Historical Context

Before Modi's tenure, India's foreign policy was characterized by non-alignment and strategic autonomy, focusing on South-South cooperation, maintaining a balanced relationship with major powers, and a cautious approach towards its neighbors. The shift or continuation in strategy under Modi has been marked by a more assertive posture, leveraging India's economic growth, military capabilities, and cultural diplomacy to enhance its global footprint.

Modi's foreign policy has been notable for its high-level engagement with the world's major powers, a more robust approach to Pakistan and China, and a significant push towards regional integration through initiatives like the Act East policy.

This introduction sets the stage for understanding the depth of India's foreign policy recalibration under Modi's leadership, emphasizing a clear departure or intensification of certain aspects of its traditional stance. The narrative will next explore how these ambitions and historical contexts have translated into specific strategies and partnerships, shaping India's place on the world stage.

Deepen into the United States Strategic Partnership

The strategic partnership between India and the United States has undergone significant transformation and deepening under Narendra Modi's leadership.

This relationship is a cornerstone of India's foreign policy, reflecting both nations' shared interests in maintaining a free, open, and inclusive Indo-Pacific region, combating terrorism, and promoting a rules-based international order.

Defense Sales and Military Cooperation

The defense relationship between India and the U.S. has reached unprecedented levels, with India purchasing over $20 billion in defense equipment from the U.S. since 2008. Notable acquisitions include C-17 Globemaster and C-130J Super Hercules transport aircraft, P-8I Poseidon maritime patrol aircraft, and AH-64E Apache and CH-47F Chinook helicopters. These purchases reflect India's intent to diversify its military procurement and enhance its strategic capabilities, particularly in the Indian Ocean region.

Military cooperation has also expanded through joint exercises, intelligence sharing, and logistics agreements such as the Logistics Exchange Memorandum of Agreement (LEMOA), the Communications Compatibility and Security Agreement (COMCASA), and the Basic Exchange and Cooperation Agreement (BECA). These agreements enhance interoperability between the two militaries and facilitate broader strategic collaboration.

Impact on Indo-Pacific Security Dynamics

The U.S.-India strategic partnership is pivotal to the Indo-Pacific security architecture. Both nations share concerns over China's assertive behavior in the region and its implications for freedom of navigation and territorial integrity. The Quadrilateral Security Dialogue (Quad), comprising the U.S., India, Japan, and Australia, has been revitalized under Modi, focusing on ensuring a free and open Indo-Pacific, enhancing maritime security, and promoting resilient supply chains.

This partnership extends beyond security, encompassing technology, healthcare, space, and climate change cooperation. The U.S. has emerged as a vital partner in India's quest for advanced technologies, including defense, information technology, and energy.

India's deepening strategic and defense ties with the U.S. under Modi's leadership underscore a mutual recognition of the importance of their partnership in addressing global challenges and ensuring regional stability. This relationship is emblematic of India's broader global strategy, seeking to enhance its international standing and security through strategic partnerships.

Explore the India-Russia Relationship

The India-Russia relationship has been a cornerstone of India's foreign policy for decades, characterized by deep-rooted strategic, military, and energy ties. Despite the shifting global alliances and India's growing closeness with the United States, the partnership with Russia remains robust, underpinned by a long history of trust and cooperation.

Arms Trade and Defense Cooperation

Russia has been India's largest and most significant defense supplier since the Cold War era, accounting for around 60% of India's defense equipment. Major acquisitions from Russia include the S-400 Triumf air defense missile systems, Sukhoi Su-30MKI fighters, and T-90 tanks.

The defense relationship extends beyond mere transactions, encompassing joint development and production initiatives such as the BrahMos missile system, reflecting a high level of trust and strategic partnership.

Energy Cooperation

Energy is another critical pillar of the India-Russia partnership. Russia is a significant oil and natural gas source for India, which is crucial for India's energy security. The two countries have long-term agreements, with Russian companies investing in India's energy sector and vice versa. Projects like Sakhalin-1 in Russia, where Indian companies have a substantial stake, exemplify this cooperation.

Balancing Relations with Western Partners

As India navigates its relationship with Western powers, particularly the United States, balancing its ties with Russia presents a diplomatic challenge. India has managed to maintain its strategic autonomy, deepening ties with the West while ensuring its relationship with Russia remains unaffected. This balance is crucial for India, given Russia's historical reliability as a defense supplier and its role as a key energy provider.

The India-Russia relationship demonstrates India's ability to maintain and cultivate strategic partnerships based on mutual interests and historical ties, even as global dynamics evolve. This partnership ensures India's defense and energy security and contributes to a multipolar world order that India aspires to promote.

Analyze the Complexities of the India-China Relationship

The India-China relationship is marked by a complex interplay of competition, cooperation, and conflict, reflecting the broader dynamics of Asian geopolitics and global power shifts. Under Narendra Modi's leadership, this relationship has seen significant developments, with strategic implications for both countries and the broader region.

Border Disputes

The long-standing border dispute is one of the most contentious aspects of the India-China relationship. Tensions flared up significantly in 2020 in the Galwan Valley, leading to a military standoff that resulted in casualties on both sides—the first in over four decades.

This incident underscored the volatile nature of India-China border issues and prompted a reevaluation of India's strategic posture towards China, emphasizing the need for strengthening border infrastructure and enhancing military readiness.

Economic Competition and Cooperation

Despite the border tensions, India and China share a significant economic relationship. China is one of India's largest trading partners, with trade encompassing a wide range of goods, including electronics, pharmaceuticals, and machinery. However, the trade imbalance in favor of China and concerns over security and privacy have led India to impose restrictions on Chinese investments and ban several Chinese apps, reflecting the broader global concerns over dependence on Chinese technology and supply chains.

In cooperation, both countries are part of multilateral forums like BRICS and the Shanghai Cooperation Organization (SCO), where they collaborate on issues of mutual interest, such as economic development and counter-terrorism. These forums provide a platform for dialogue and engagement, counterbalancing their bilateral tensions.

Efforts to Manage Tensions

India's approach to managing its complex relationship with China involves a combination of strategic patience, diplomatic engagement, and military preparedness.

Modi's administration has emphasized the importance of dialogue, as seen in his meetings with Chinese President Xi Jinping, to stabilize relations and establish mechanisms to resolve disputes peacefully. However, India has also been diversifying its economic and strategic partnerships, as evidenced by closer ties with the United States, Japan, Australia, and other Indo-Pacific nations, to counterbalance China's growing influence.

The India-China relationship under Modi thus reflects a delicate balancing act, navigating between competition and cooperation, with significant implications for regional stability and global geopolitics. This complexity underscores India's challenges in securing its interests while engaging with a rising China.

Detail the 'Neighbourhood First' Policy's Impact on South Asia

The 'Neighbourhood First' policy is a cornerstone of Narendra Modi's foreign policy, reflecting India's strategic imperative to foster stable, friendly, and mutually beneficial relations with its immediate neighbors. This policy prioritizes India's immediate neighborhood in its diplomatic engagements and development strategy, aiming to build a shared environment of trust and cooperation.

Enhancing Connectivity

One of the key focuses of the 'Neighbourhood First' policy has been enhancing connectivity with neighboring countries through infrastructure development, including roads, railways, waterways, and energy grids. Projects like the India-Myanmar-Thailand Trilateral Highway, the Bangladesh-Bhutan-India-Nepal (BBIN) Initiative, and the development of the Chabahar Port in Iran are aimed at facilitating trade, improving access, and strengthening economic integration in the region.

Economic Aid and Development Projects

India has significantly increased its economic aid and investment in neighboring countries, financing various development projects, from Bhutan and Nepal hydroelectric power plants to the Afghanistan Parliament Building. These initiatives are designed to bolster economic development in the region and counterbalance China's expanding influence through its Belt and Road Initiative.

Resolving Long-standing Issues

The Modi administration has tried to resolve longstanding issues with its neighbors, such as the land boundary agreement with Bangladesh, which resolved a decades-old border dispute. Similarly, India has engaged in high-level dialogues with Sri Lanka to address ethnic reconciliation and with Nepal to resolve border disputes, although these efforts have faced challenges and criticism.

Impact and Challenges

The 'Neighbourhood First' policy has had mixed results. While India has made strides in improving relations and connectivity with countries like Bangladesh and Bhutan, it has faced challenges in dealing with Nepal and Sri Lanka, where India's intentions and projects have sometimes been viewed with suspicion. China's growing economic and strategic footprint in South Asia also challenges the policy's success, requiring India to navigate a delicate balance of influence and cooperation in its backyard.

Overall, the 'Neighbourhood First' policy underscores India's strategic commitment to its immediate neighborhood, recognizing the importance of regional stability and cooperation for its security and prosperity. However, the effectiveness of this policy continues to be tested by geopolitical dynamics and domestic politics within South Asian countries.

Assess India's Leadership in Global Climate Action Initiatives

Under Prime Minister Narendra Modi's leadership, India has positioned itself as a pivotal player in global climate action, emphasizing its commitment to sustainable development and energy transition. This leadership is manifested in various initiatives and commitments that aim to meet India's ambitious environmental targets and encourage global cooperation in combating climate change.

International Solar Alliance (ISA)

One of the hallmark initiatives of India's climate action has been the establishment of the International Solar Alliance (ISA) in 2015 in partnership with France. The ISA aims to mobilize efforts among solar-rich countries located between the Tropic of Cancer and the Tropic of Capricorn to harness solar energy and reduce dependence on fossil fuels. With over 120 countries joining the alliance, ISA exemplifies India's leadership in fostering global collaboration towards a sustainable and clean energy future.

Commitments Under the Paris Agreement

India's Nationally Determined Contributions (NDCs) under the Paris Agreement reflect its serious commitment to climate action. Despite its developmental challenges, India has pledged to reduce the emissions intensity of its GDP by 33-35% by 2030 from 2005 levels, to achieve about 40% cumulative electric power installed capacity from non-fossil fuel-based energy resources, and to create an additional carbon sink of 2.5 to 3 billion tonnes of CO_2 equivalent through forest and tree cover by 2030. India's progress in increasing its renewable energy capacity, especially in solar and wind energy, highlights its efforts to meet these ambitious goals.

Leadership in Global Climate Dialogues

India has actively participated in and sometimes led major international climate negotiations, advocating for the principles of equity and common but differentiated responsibilities (CBDR). Modi's administration has emphasized the need for developed countries to fulfill their climate finance commitments, arguing that significant financial and technological support is essential for developing countries to achieve their climate goals. India's approach to climate change under Modi has been characterized by a blend of domestic initiatives aimed at energy transition and international advocacy for justice and equity in global climate action.

This dual approach underscores the complexities of addressing climate change in a developing country, where economic growth and environmental sustainability must be balanced. India's leadership in global climate initiatives, especially the International Solar Alliance, showcases its commitment to playing a significant role in the global fight against climate change, aligning its development objectives with environmental sustainability.

Explore India's Role in Multilateral Organizations

India's engagement with multilateral organizations under Prime Minister Narendra Modi has been characterized by a proactive and assertive approach to enhance India's global standing and influence international discourse on key issues, including reform of global governance, counter-terrorism, climate change, and economic development.

United Nations (UN)

India has long advocated for reform of the United Nations, especially the Security Council, seeking greater representation for emerging economies and developing nations to reflect the current global dynamics more accurately. Modi's administration has emphasized this position in various international forums, calling for a more democratic, transparent, and effective UN that responds to the challenges of the 21st century. India's election to a non-permanent seat on the United Nations Security Council for the 2021-2022 term exemplifies its commitment to playing a more active role in global governance.

G20 and Economic Diplomacy

India's participation in the G20 has been a key aspect of its economic diplomacy, with Modi using the platform to advocate for issues critical to developing countries, such as financial inclusivity, sustainable development, and global economic governance reforms. India's role in the G20 underlines its position as a major global economic player and its readiness to contribute to shaping the global economic agenda.

BRICS and South-South Cooperation

As a founding member of BRICS (Brazil, Russia, India, China, and South Africa), India has leveraged this platform to promote South-South cooperation and advocate for a more equitable global order. BRICS serves as an important counterbalance to Western-dominated global institutions, and Modi has used this forum to push for greater economic and political cooperation among developing countries, highlighting India's leadership in the Global South.

Challenges and Opportunities

While India has sought to enhance its role in multilateral organizations, it faces challenges, including balancing its strategic interests with those of other major powers, addressing the concerns of its neighbors, and managing the expectations of its domestic and international stakeholders. Nonetheless, these platforms offer India significant opportunities to project its soft power, negotiate trade and climate agreements, and advocate for international terrorism and security reforms.

India's active participation in multilateral organizations under Modi's leadership underscores its aspiration to be a leading voice in global affairs, reflecting its ambition to play a central role in shaping the international order in the 21st century.

Reflect on Modi's Foreign Policy Legacy and Future Directions

Prime Minister Narendra Modi's tenure has marked a significant phase in India's foreign policy, characterized by continuity and change. Modi's assertive approach, aimed at elevating India's global stature, has been underpinned by strategic partnerships, a focus on the Indo-Pacific region, and active engagement in global governance.

Achievements and Challenges

Modi's foreign policy achievements include strengthening strategic ties with major powers like the United States, revitalizing the Quad to counter China in the Indo-Pacific, and pioneering global initiatives such as the International Solar Alliance. Despite facing challenges, his 'Neighbourhood First' policy has underscored the importance of regional stability and cooperation for India's security and development.

However, Modi's foreign policy has not been without its controversies and challenges. The border standoff with China has tested India's strategic patience and military preparedness, highlighting the complexities of its relationship with Beijing. Relations with Pakistan remain fraught, with terrorism and Kashmir continuing to be major sticking points. Moreover, balancing deepening ties with the U.S. and its allies with traditional relationships, notably with Russia, poses a diplomatic challenge amidst shifting global alliances.

Future Directions

Modi's foreign policy will likely continue enhancing India's strategic autonomy, ensuring national security, and pursuing economic growth through global engagement. This may involve diversifying energy sources, investing in defense capabilities, and expanding digital infrastructure to enhance India's competitive edge.

India's role in shaping the post-pandemic world order will be crucial, particularly regarding global health governance and economic recovery. The *Vaccine Maitri* initiative has set a precedent for India's leadership in global health diplomacy, a role likely to expand in the coming years.

India's Role in a Changing World Order

As the world grapples with shifting power dynamics, climate change, and technological disruptions, India's place in the global order is poised to evolve.

Modi's vision of a self-reliant India, democratic values, demographic dividend, and economic potential position the country as a key player in addressing global challenges.

India's emphasis on multilateralism, climate action, and digital innovation will be instrumental in fostering global cooperation and sustainable development. By balancing its strategic interests with global responsibilities, India, under Modi's leadership, is navigating a path towards greater global influence and leadership.

In conclusion, Narendra Modi's foreign policy legacy is marked by a proactive approach to diplomacy, strategic recalibrations, and a vision for India's elevated role in global affairs. As India continues to assert its place on the world stage, its contributions to global governance, peace, and development will be critical in shaping the future international order.

This chapter comprehensively explains India's foreign policy under Narendra Modi, highlighting key strategic partnerships, regional dynamics, and contributions to global issues. Through a balanced exploration of achievements and challenges, the narrative offers insights into India's aspirations and realities on the world stage, setting the context for discussions on the country's future directions in international relations.

CHAPTER 15

LEGACY IN THE MAKING

"The true measure of our success will not be in the achievements of today, but
In the legacy we leave for generations to come.
It's a future built on the foundations of
growth, inclusivity, and sustainability."

— Narendra Modi

Speculating on the lasting impact of Narendra Modi's tenure, this chapter contemplates the trajectory of India's future development. It discusses the potential legacies of Modi's policies, leadership, and vision, exploring how these elements might shape the nation's destiny in the years to come.

Introduction Detail

The final chapter, "Legacy in the Making," begins by setting the stage for evaluating a political leader's legacy. It's crucial to understand the weight such an assessment carries, especially when the leader in question is Narendra Modi, a figure who has elicited strong reactions across the spectrum of Indian and international opinion.

Modi's tenure as Prime Minister of India has been marked by significant shifts in the country's socio-political and economic landscapes, driven by a vision that promised to reshape India's destiny.

Modi's vision for India, as articulated over his years in office, is anchored in three core themes: development, nationalism, and asserting India's place as a leader on the global stage. These themes have guided his policy decisions and fueled a transformative agenda to elevate India's economic status, redefine its cultural identity, and enhance its geopolitical influence.

This section recaps the ambitious goals Modi set forth, underlining the initiatives to accelerate economic growth, promote a sense of national pride rooted in cultural heritage, and position India as a formidable player in international affairs. The introduction lays a foundation for the ensuing analysis, preparing readers to delve into the complexities of Modi's policies, their impacts, and the lasting changes they may imprint on India's fabric.

By navigating through these themes, the chapter offers a nuanced perspective on the Modi era, balancing the achievements against the criticisms and controversies that have also marked his tenure. This approach sets the tone for an in-depth exploration of the legacy Modi is poised to leave behind, a legacy that will undoubtedly shape India's trajectory for years to come.

Long-term Impact of Economic Policies

The economic landscape under Narendra Modi has been characterized by bold and, at times, controversial reforms aimed at restructuring India's economy. Two of the most significant policies—the demonetization of high-value currency notes in November 2016 and the implementation of the Goods and Services Tax (GST) in July 2017—serve as focal points for evaluating the long-term impacts of Modi's economic strategies.

Demonetization was introduced to curb black money, reduce counterfeit currency, and promote digital transactions. While it led to a temporary disruption in economic activities and faced criticism for its immediate impact on the informal sector, its long-term effects have been a matter of extensive debate. Supporters argue that demonetization has helped widen the tax base and accelerate the adoption of digital payments, thereby formalizing the economy to a greater extent. Critics, however, point to the loss of jobs and the slowdown in GDP growth in the subsequent quarters as evidence of its negative repercussions.

On the other hand, GST aims to unify India's complex tax structure into a single, streamlined system, enhancing the ease of doing business and ensuring better tax compliance. While its implementation faced teething problems, including technical glitches and confusion over tax slabs, the long-term perspective appears more favorable. GST has the potential to significantly boost economic efficiency, reduce the cost of goods and services, and increase government revenues in the long run.

Analyzing these economic reforms reveals a pattern of ambitious attempts to transform India's economic framework. While the immediate fallout of some policies stirred controversy and debate, their intended long-term benefits include a more inclusive and formalized economic system, enhanced tax compliance, and a push toward digitalization. However, the balance between these policies' intended outcomes and the on-ground realities continues to be a subject of rigorous analysis and discussion.

These economic transformations under Modi's leadership reflect a broader agenda of reshaping India's economic destiny. As we project into the future, the enduring impact of these policies on India's economy will be a critical aspect of Modi's legacy, offering insights into the effectiveness of bold economic reforms in driving sustainable growth and development.

Industrial and Technological Advancements

Under Narendra Modi's leadership, India has embarked on a path toward significant industrial and technological advancements, with initiatives like "Make in India" and "Digital India" sitting at the forefront of this journey. These programs have been designed to position India as a global manufacturing hub and to digitize government and financial services, aiming to foster inclusive growth by leveraging technology.

Make in India was launched in September 2014 to encourage national and multinational companies to manufacture their products in India. This initiative seeks to boost job creation, enhance skill development, and promote innovation across multiple sectors, including automobiles, textiles, pharmaceuticals, and electronics. Focusing on high-quality standards and minimizing bureaucratic hurdles, "Make in India" aims to attract foreign investment and increase India's share in global manufacturing.

The long-term impact of "Make in India" is anticipated to be transformative, potentially elevating India's manufacturing sector, increasing exports, and generating millions of jobs. However, the success of this initiative depends on the sustained implementation of reforms that improve the ease of doing business, infrastructure development, and labor laws.

Digital India, another flagship initiative, was launched in July 2015 to transform India into a digitally empowered society and knowledge economy. It encompasses many projects to ensure government services are available to citizens electronically, improve digital infrastructure, and increase internet connectivity, especially in rural areas. Digital India has led to significant achievements, including the expansion of mobile connectivity, the proliferation of digital payment platforms, and the establishment of a unique identity system through Aadhaar, enabling direct benefit transfers and reduced leakages in subsidy programs.

The future of India's industrial sector and technological innovation looks promising, with "Make in India" and "Digital India" laying the groundwork for a modernized economy. These initiatives are expected to drive India's transition towards high-value manufacturing and a digitally enabled society, contributing significantly to the country's economic growth and global competitiveness.

The trajectory of India's development in these areas will be a crucial component of Narendra Modi's legacy, reflecting his administration's efforts to harness technology and industrialization as engines of economic transformation. As we look ahead, the continued evolution of these initiatives will play a pivotal role in shaping India's economic landscape and its position on the world stage.

Welfare and Social Justice

The tenure of Narendra Modi has been marked by a significant emphasis on welfare schemes and social justice initiatives aimed at improving the lives of India's most vulnerable populations. These programs cover a broad spectrum, from financial inclusion and affordable housing to healthcare and education, reflecting an integrated approach to fostering social welfare and reducing inequality.

Financial Inclusion and Empowerment: One of the flagship initiatives in this domain is the Pradhan Mantri Jan Dhan Yojana (PMJDY), launched in August 2014 to provide universal access to banking services.

This program has been instrumental in opening millions of bank accounts for the unbanked population, facilitating direct benefit transfers, and ensuring financial inclusion. PMJDY has laid the foundation for more inclusive economic growth by connecting the previously unbanked to the formal financial system.

Healthcare: The Ayushman Bharat scheme, introduced in September 2018, aims to provide health insurance to over 500 million individuals, making it one of the world's largest health insurance schemes. This initiative seeks to address the healthcare needs of the poor and vulnerable, offering financial protection against health-related expenditures and improving access to quality health services.

Housing and Sanitation: The Pradhan Mantri Awas Yojana (PMAY) and the Swachh Bharat Mission (SBM) have been pivotal in promoting affordable housing and improving sanitation nationwide. PMAY aims to provide affordable housing to the urban and rural poor by 2022, while SBM focuses on eliminating open defecation through the construction of toilets promoting cleanliness and hygiene.

These welfare initiatives represent a concerted effort to address the multifaceted challenges of poverty, health insecurity, and inadequate housing. The potential long-term benefits of these schemes include improved health outcomes, enhanced financial stability, and reduced poverty levels. However, the effective implementation and sustained impact of these programs remain areas of focus, requiring continuous monitoring and adaptation to meet the evolving needs of India's population.

Challenges and Criticisms: While these initiatives have received commendation for their ambitious scope and potential impact, they have also faced challenges in implementation, including issues related to coverage, delivery mechanisms, and financial sustainability. Critiques often highlight the gap between policy intent and on-ground execution, emphasizing the need for strengthening institutional capacities and ensuring that the benefits reach the intended beneficiaries.

As we look toward the future, the legacy of Modi's welfare and social justice initiatives will be measured by their ability to bring about tangible improvements in the lives of India's most disadvantaged citizens.

The long-term success of these programs will significantly influence India's socio-economic fabric, potentially serving as a model for comprehensive welfare-oriented governance.

National Identity and Cultural Discourse

Prime Minister Narendra Modi's tenure has been characterized by a pronounced emphasis on reinforcing national identity and reshaping cultural discourse in India. This focus has been articulated through various initiatives and narratives that stress traditional values, cultural heritage, and a sense of national pride. While these efforts have garnered widespread support for fostering a stronger sense of identity among Indians, they have also sparked debates regarding their implications for India's pluralistic society.

Promotion of Cultural Heritage: Modi's government has actively promoted India's rich cultural and historical heritage, emphasizing the country's ancient traditions, languages, and practices. Initiatives like the International Day of Yoga, the revival and internationalization of Ayurveda, and the enhancement of historical site preservation aim to showcase India's contributions to the world and instill pride in Indian citizens.

Cultural Nationalism: A significant aspect of Modi's approach to national identity is the promotion of cultural nationalism, which seeks to prioritize Indian traditions and values as central to the nation's identity. This has been evident in educational reforms, changes to the curriculum to include more content on Indian culture and history and the celebration of Hindu festivals and figures at a national level. While this has been praised for enriching national pride, critics argue it risks marginalizing minority cultures and viewpoints within India's diverse society.

Language Policies: Efforts to promote Hindi and Sanskrit as central to India's cultural identity have been part of the broader agenda to reinforce a cohesive national narrative. These efforts aim to elevate the status of Indian languages, but they have also led to concerns among speakers of other regional languages about the potential diminishment of their linguistic heritage.

Implications for Pluralism: The emphasis on a singular national identity raises questions about the inclusivity of India's multicultural and multi-religious society. Critics contend that the push towards a unified cultural narrative may overlook the country's diversity, potentially alienating minority groups and contributing to social divisions. The impact of these cultural and nationalistic endeavors on India's national identity and cultural discourse is profound, with long-term implications for societal cohesion and the balance between unity and diversity. As India moves forward, the challenge lies in nurturing a sense of national pride that embraces the country's rich tapestry of cultures, languages, and religions, ensuring that the national identity narrative is inclusive and representative of all Indians. The legacy of Modi's tenure in this regard will be closely watched, as it will influence the current socio-cultural landscape and how future generations perceive and value India's pluralistic heritage.

Sustainability and Climate Leadership

In the era of Narendra Modi, India has taken significant strides towards establishing itself as a sustainability and climate action leader. Modi's government has greatly emphasized balancing economic development with environmental stewardship, recognizing the critical importance of sustainable practices for the future of the country and the planet. This commitment is evident in India's participation in international climate agreements, the launch of ambitious renewable energy initiatives, and efforts to incorporate sustainability across various sectors of the economy.

Renewable Energy Initiatives: A cornerstone of India's approach to sustainability has been the aggressive pursuit of renewable energy sources. The government has set ambitious targets for renewable energy capacity, aiming to reach 175 GW by 2022 and further extending this goal to 450 GW by 2030. This includes significant investments in solar and wind energy, exemplified by establishing the International Solar Alliance (ISA), co-founded by India, to promote solar energy globally.

These initiatives reduce carbon emissions and signal India's commitment to leading by example in the transition towards a green economy.

Environmental Policies: Beyond renewable energy, Modi's government has implemented various policies for conservation, water resource management, and pollution reduction. The Swachh Bharat Mission, while primarily a sanitation and hygiene initiative, also contributes to environmental sustainability by addressing waste management issues. Similarly, projects like the Namami Gange Programme, aimed at cleaning and conserving the Ganga river, highlight the administration's focus on water conservation and habitat restoration.

Global Climate Leadership: India's active participation in international climate discussions, including the Paris Agreement, positions the country as a vital player in global sustainability efforts. Modi's advocacy for climate action reflects an understanding of India's role as a major emitter and a vulnerable nation facing significant climate change impacts. By championing the cause of developing nations and emphasizing equity in climate action, Modi's approach underscores the need for collective responsibility and cooperation in addressing global environmental challenges.

Challenges and Criticisms: Despite these efforts, India faces ongoing challenges in its sustainability journey, including balancing economic growth with environmental protection, addressing air and water pollution, and ensuring equitable access to clean energy.

Critics argue for more robust measures to combat pollution and for greater emphasis on sustainability in urban planning and industrial practices. As India projects its future development trajectory, the sustainability and climate leadership demonstrated during Modi's tenure will be a defining aspect of his legacy. The success of these initiatives in achieving long-term environmental goals and fostering a sustainable development model will have lasting implications for India's economy, people, and role on the global stage.

India's Position on the World Stage

Under Prime Minister Narendra Modi, India has notably shifted its position and influence on the global stage, pursuing an active foreign policy aimed at enhancing its geopolitical standing and fostering strategic partnerships. Modi's tenure has been marked by a robust approach to diplomacy, leveraging India's economic growth, cultural heritage, and democratic values to assert its role as a major world power.

Strategic Partnerships and Alliances: One of the hallmarks of Modi's foreign policy has been cultivating closer ties with key global powers, including the United States, European Union, Japan, and Australia while maintaining a complex relationship with neighboring China and Pakistan. The emphasis on the Quad alliance (comprising the USA, India, Japan, and Australia) underscores India's commitment to playing a pivotal role in Indo-Pacific security and economic cooperation, countering China's assertive presence in the region.

Economic Diplomacy: Modi has skillfully used India's growing economy as a tool for diplomacy, engaging in trade negotiations, investment initiatives, and technology partnerships. The Make in India campaign has also been a significant aspect of this strategy, attracting foreign investment and showcasing India as a manufacturing and innovation hub.

Climate Change and Sustainability: On the environmental front, Modi has positioned India as a leader in climate action, advocating for sustainable development and global cooperation in forums such as the United Nations and G20. The International Solar Alliance initiative reflects India's commitment to leading by example in the transition towards renewable energy.

Cultural Diplomacy: Modi's government has leveraged India's rich cultural heritage and diaspora to strengthen international ties, promoting yoga, Ayurveda, and Bollywood as elements of soft power that enhance India's global image and influence.

Challenges and Critiques: Despite these achievements, India's foreign policy under Modi faces challenges, including managing tensions with Pakistan and China, addressing regional stability issues, and navigating the complexities of global trade and environmental agreements. Critiques often focus on a more nuanced approach to balancing strategic interests with democratic values and human rights concerns. As India continues to assert its position on the world stage, the strategies adopted during Modi's tenure will impact its global relationships and influence. The legacy of this period in India's foreign policy will be evaluated based on how successfully it has managed to enhance its global standing while addressing internal and external challenges.

Addressing Unresolved Issues

While Narendra Modi's tenure as Prime Minister has been marked by significant achievements and ambitious initiatives, it has also faced its share of challenges and unresolved issues. These encompass concerns over democratic practices, secularism, economic disparities, environmental sustainability, and social harmony. Addressing these issues is crucial for India's continued growth and stability, highlighting areas where further efforts are needed to align Modi's legacy with the aspirations of all segments of Indian society.

Democratic Practices and Press Freedom: Critics have raised concerns about the health of democracy in India, citing instances of curtailed press freedom, challenges to the independence of institutions, and restrictions on civil society organizations. The balancing act between national security and preserving democratic freedoms remains a contentious issue, with advocates calling for greater transparency and protection of civil liberties.

Secularism and Social Harmony: Modi's tenure has seen debates intensify around India's secular fabric, with policies and rhetoric accused of favoring majoritarianism at the expense of minority rights. The revocation of Article 370 in Jammu and Kashmir, the implementation of the Citizenship Amendment Act (CAA), and incidents of communal violence have sparked discussions about inclusivity and equality before the law. Ongoing challenges include fostering social cohesion and ensuring that policies are perceived as fair and inclusive.

Economic Disparities: India grapples with significant economic disparities despite notable economic reforms and growth. Rural distress, unemployment, and the impact of COVID-19 on small businesses and informal workers highlight the need for focused economic policies that ensure equitable growth and social security for the vulnerable.

Environmental Concerns: While India has made strides in renewable energy and sustainability, environmental degradation and pollution remain pressing concerns. Balancing economic development with environmental protection, managing water resources, and combating air pollution are critical areas requiring sustained attention and innovative solutions.

Future Pathways: Addressing these unresolved issues involves a multipronged approach, including policy refinement, strengthening institutions, fostering dialogue and reconciliation, and prioritizing sustainable development.

Modi's administration and future governments must navigate these challenges thoughtfully, ensuring that India's growth is inclusive, democratic, and sustainable. As India looks toward the future, resolving these issues will significantly influence the country's trajectory, shaping the legacy of Modi's tenure and the nation's ability to achieve its full potential.

Defining Modi's Legacy

Narendra Modi's tenure as Prime Minister of India is marked by ambitious visions, transformative policies, and a strong push towards asserting India's position on the global stage. However, it is also a tenure that has not been without its controversies and challenges. Defining Modi's legacy, therefore, involves a nuanced examination of the achievements and criticisms that have characterized his years in office.

Achievements: Modi's leadership has been defined by bold economic reforms, such as the Goods and Services Tax (GST) and the push for digital transactions through demonetization, aiming to streamline the economy and reduce corruption. Initiatives like "Make in India," "Digital India," and significant investments in renewable energy have sought to modernize the Indian economy and prepare it for the future. On the international front, Modi has reinvigorated India's foreign policy, fostering strategic partnerships and positioning India as a key player in global affairs, particularly in climate change advocacy.

Criticisms: Despite these achievements, Modi's tenure has faced criticism over issues such as the handling of the demonetization exercise, the implementation of the Citizenship Amendment Act (CAA), and the revocation of Article 370 in Jammu and Kashmir, which have sparked debates about economic impact, secularism, and democratic freedoms. Additionally, concerns regarding environmental sustainability and social harmony have been points of contention, highlighting the complex challenges of governing a diverse and populous nation like India.

The Balance of Perspectives: Modi's legacy will likely be viewed through a lens that balances these achievements and criticisms. For supporters, his tenure represents decisive leadership, economic reform, and national pride. For critics, it raises concerns about democratic practices, minority rights, and social cohesion.

Impact on Future Governance: The policies and leadership style of Narendra Modi will undoubtedly influence future political leaders and governance models in India. His emphasis on digitalization, economic reform, and proactive foreign policy sets a precedent that future administrations may follow or react against. Moreover, the debates about democracy, secularism, and economic policy sparked during his tenure will continue to shape political discourse. As India moves forward, the legacy of Modi's tenure will be a subject of ongoing evaluation, reflecting the complexities of governance in one of the world's largest and most diverse democracies. The true measure of this legacy will be seen in how the initiatives and policies introduced during his time in office continue to impact India's socio-political and economic landscape in the years to come.

The Road Ahead for India

As Narendra Modi's tenure unfolds, India's road is paved with challenges and opportunities. The groundwork laid during his leadership sets the stage for future development and highlights areas requiring continued attention and innovation. The trajectory of India's growth and its role on the global stage will be shaped by how these challenges are addressed and how the opportunities are leveraged.

Economic Growth and Inclusion: A key focus for India moving forward will be to sustain economic growth while ensuring that it is inclusive and benefits all sections of society. Addressing unemployment, supporting small and medium enterprises (SMEs), and fostering innovation are critical to creating a robust economy.

The emphasis on digital infrastructure and technology can catalyze new economic opportunities, bridging the rural-urban divide and enhancing access to services and markets.

Social Harmony and Inclusivity: The fabric of India's society, with its rich diversity, requires nurturing to ensure social harmony and inclusivity. Policies and discourse that promote unity without erasing diversity will be crucial in maintaining India's pluralistic identity. Addressing social and economic disparities, ensuring justice and equal opportunities for minority communities, and fostering a culture of tolerance and dialogue is imperative for social cohesion.

Environmental Sustainability: As one of the most vulnerable countries to climate change impacts, India's commitment to environmental sustainability and climate action will remain a priority. Balancing development needs with environmental protection, investing in renewable energy, and leading global initiatives on climate change are essential for sustainable development and securing a healthy planet for future generations.

Global Leadership and Diplomacy: India's evolving role on the world stage involves not just economic and military strength but also leadership in global governance, particularly in areas like climate change, technology, and healthcare. Navigating complex geopolitical landscapes, building strategic partnerships, and advocating for equity in global institutions will define India's global leadership in the coming years.

Reflective Thoughts on India's Potential: The path India chooses to take, inspired by the policies and vision set forth by Narendra Modi and subsequent leaders, will influence its potential to emerge as a global power that is economically prosperous, socially inclusive, and environmentally sustainable. Leadership, policy continuity, and active citizen engagement will play pivotal roles in shaping India's future.

As India looks ahead, its challenges are as significant as the opportunities. The nation's journey towards realizing its full potential will be a testament to its people's resilience, innovation, and spirit.

Conclusion and Call to Action

As we conclude this chapter on "Legacy in the Making," it's clear that Narendra Modi's tenure as Prime Minister has been a significant transformation for India. Through a combination of ambitious policies, visionary leadership, and a strong push towards asserting India's position on the global stage, Modi has left an indelible mark on the country's socio-political and economic fabric. However, his legacy is also intertwined with the challenges and controversies that have sparked intense debate and reflection across Indian society.

The Complexity of Legacy: Modi's legacy is a testament to the complexity of governing a diverse and dynamic nation like India. It encapsulates the achievements in economic reform, digitalization, and global diplomacy while confronting unresolved issues related to social harmony, environmental sustainability, and democratic values. This duality invites a nuanced understanding of leadership and its impact on a nation's trajectory.

India's Future Trajectory: Looking ahead, the future of India appears both promising and challenging. The groundwork laid during Modi's tenure provides a blueprint for continued growth and development, but it also highlights the critical areas where sustained effort and innovation are required. The road ahead for India will demand a balanced approach to economic development, social equity, and environmental stewardship.

A Call to Action: This chapter, and the broader narrative of India's future, is a reflection on leadership and a call to action for all stakeholders in Indian society. Policymakers, citizens, businesses, and the international community each have a role to play in shaping India's trajectory.

Engaging in informed dialogue, participating in democratic processes, and contributing to sustainable development are essential for realizing the vision of a prosperous, inclusive, and forward-looking India.

Reflective Thoughts on India's Potential: As we contemplate the various paths India might take, it's evident that the nation's potential is boundless. Inspired by the policies and vision set forth by Modi, as well as the contributions of countless others, India stands on the cusp of a new era. The choices made today will determine the legacy of future generations, making it imperative to foster leadership, policy continuity, and civic engagement.

In closing, "Legacy in the Making" invites readers to reflect on the past and present and actively engage with the narrative of India's future. It's a call to envision a path that honors the achievements of the past while boldly addressing the challenges of the future, ensuring that the legacy of leadership advances the well-being and aspirations of all Indians.

This chapter aims to encapsulate the complex legacy of Narendra Modi's tenure, balancing transformative aspirations and achievements with critiques and challenges. Through this exploration, readers are provided with a comprehensive understanding of Modi's impact on India, setting the stage for informed contemplation and discussion about the country's future trajectory and the enduring legacy of its current leadership.

CONCLUSION

THE ROAD AHEAD FOR MODI'S INDIA

"India is not just a geographical entity. It is a great idea, a vision, and a living cultural and civilizational heritage."

— Narendra Modi

A synthesis of Modi's vision, the transformation under his leadership, and contemplation of the enduring challenges and opportunities that lie ahead. This concluding chapter reflects on the narrative of change that has defined Modi's India, pondering the complexities, achievements, and uncharted paths that lie ahead for the nation.

Introduction

Recapitulation: Narendra Modi's leadership has significantly transformed India, marked by ambitious initiatives to propel the country towards modernization and global standing. From implementing the Goods and Services Tax (GST) to the push for digital India, his tenure has seen efforts to reshape India's economic landscape, societal norms, and international relations.

The Vision Revisited: Modi's vision for India has consistently emphasized development, nationalism, and elevating India's global stature. Through policies, speeches, and initiatives, Modi has articulated a future for India that combines economic growth with technological innovation, aiming for a country that not only thrives internally but also commands respect internationally.

Economic Growth and Challenges

The economic landscape under Modi's leadership has been characterized by bold reforms intended to streamline the economy, enhance transparency, and foster sustainable growth. The introduction of the Goods and Services Tax (GST) sought to unify the country's fragmented tax system, promoting a more integrated economy. Digitalization efforts, notably the Digital India initiative, aimed to increase access to government services through technology, reduce corruption, and improve efficiency.

Achievements

GST Implementation: Launched in 2017, GST represented a major tax reform, aiming to simplify the complex tax structure and enhance compliance, thereby increasing revenue collection.

Digital India: This initiative has been pivotal in increasing digital literacy, promoting e-governance, and facilitating digital transactions, contributing to a less cash-dependent economy.

Infrastructure Development: Significant investments in infrastructure, from roads and railways to airports and urban development, have aimed to improve connectivity and stimulate economic growth.

Challenges

Unemployment and Sectoral Distress: Despite economic reforms, unemployment rates have remained a concern, particularly in the manufacturing and agricultural sectors.

Economic Disparities: Economic growth has also been critiqued for widening the gap between the rich and the poor, raising concerns about inclusive growth.

COVID-19 Impact: The pandemic has further exacerbated economic challenges, significantly impacting small businesses and informal workers and highlighting economic vulnerabilities.

Societal and Cultural Shifts

Modi's tenure has also witnessed significant societal and cultural shifts, with a strong emphasis on national identity and traditional values, alongside efforts to improve welfare, education, and healthcare.

Advancements

Welfare Schemes: Initiatives like the Pradhan Mantri Jan Dhan Yojana for financial inclusion and the Swachh Bharat Mission for sanitation have aimed at improving the quality of life for millions.

Education and Healthcare Reforms: Efforts to increase access to quality education and healthcare through the National Health Protection Scheme reflect a commitment to societal development.

Debates:

National Identity and Secularism: Modi's tenure has seen vigorous debates over India's national identity, with criticisms of fostering a climate that challenges the country's secular foundation.

Citizenship Amendment Act (CAA) and National Register of Citizens (NRC): These policies have sparked widespread protests and debates about inclusivity and human rights.

Environmental and Global Stance

India under Modi has taken significant strides in environmental sustainability and international diplomacy, seeking to position itself as a responsible global player.

Environmental Efforts

International Solar Alliance (ISA): Launched in 2015, the ISA aims to promote solar energy globally, showcasing India's leadership in renewable energy.

Commitment to the Paris Agreement: India has been committed to the Paris Agreement goals, working towards reducing carbon emissions and increasing the use of renewable energy sources.

Global Diplomacy

Strategic Partnerships: Modi's foreign policy has focused on strengthening strategic partnerships, notably with the United States, Japan, and countries in the Middle East, enhancing India's geopolitical influence.

Defense and Security: Enhancing defense capabilities and securing India's borders have been priorities, with increased defense spending and initiatives to indigenize defense production.

Enduring Challenges

Democracy and Governance

Significant debates over democratic processes, institutional integrity, and the balance of power have marked the governance landscape under Modi. Critics argue that there has been an erosion of democratic norms, citing actions perceived to weaken independent institutions and centralize power.

Key Issues

Institutional Autonomy: Concerns over the independence of India's judiciary, electoral bodies, and investigative agencies have been raised, with fears that their autonomy is compromised.

Media Freedom: The freedom of the press and expression has been another concern, with reports of increased censorship and pressure on media outlets to align with government perspectives.

Secularism and Social Harmony

India's secular ethos has faced challenges amidst rising communal tensions and debates over citizenship and national identity. The implementation of policies like the CAA and NRC has sparked fears of undermining secular principles and marginalizing minority communities.

Challenges

Communal Harmony: Incidents of communal violence and rhetoric have raised alarms about the impact on India's social fabric, emphasizing the need for inclusive policies and dialogue to foster unity.

Minority Rights: The protection and promotion of minority rights remain critical, with the need to balance national security concerns with the principles of equality and non-discrimination.

Economic Inequality and Sustainability

Despite progress, economic inequality and pursuing sustainable development pose significant challenges. The economic growth has not been evenly distributed, leading to disparities that threaten long-term sustainability.

Concerns

Regional Disparities: There is a stark contrast in economic development levels across different states and regions, highlighting the need for policies that promote equitable growth.

Sustainable Development: Balancing economic growth with environmental sustainability is increasingly crucial, requiring innovative approaches to ensure that development does not come at the expense of ecological balance.

Opportunities Ahead

Technological and Economic Potential

India's vibrant startup ecosystem and strong foundation in IT and digital technologies present significant opportunities for leveraging innovation for economic growth. The focus on digital infrastructure and skill development can drive India towards becoming a global hub for technology and services.

Role on the World Stage

India's strategic geopolitical position and growing economy make it more influential in global affairs. From climate change initiatives to peacekeeping and security, India has the potential to contribute significantly to shaping global policies and norms.

Societal Development

Further social welfare, healthcare, and education advancements are essential for building a more equitable and just society. The continued focus on inclusive policies and programs can ensure that the benefits of growth and development reach all sections of society.

Reflecting on Modi's Legacy

The potential legacy of Modi's tenure will be measured by the breadth of his policies, their societal impact, and the shift in India's global image. The emphasis on development, nationalism, and global prominence has redefined India's trajectory, but the enduring challenges highlight the need for ongoing effort, vigilance, and adaptation.

Conclusion

Vision for the Future: The road ahead for Modi's India is one of continued innovation, governance, and societal engagement. Building upon the foundation laid during Modi's tenure requires a collective effort toward sustaining growth, fostering inclusivity, and maintaining democratic principles.

Call to Action for Readers: The transformation of India is an ongoing process, with each citizen playing a crucial role in shaping its future. Engagement in civic activities, informed dialogue and contributions to development efforts are vital for realizing the vision of a prosperous, inclusive, and globally respected India.

Reflecting on the comprehensive analysis of "Modi's India: Vision, Transformation, & the Road Ahead," it's clear that the journey has been transformative. Yet, the path forward requires addressing enduring challenges and seizing emerging opportunities to ensure a legacy of sustainable and inclusive growth.

REFLECTIVE THOUGHTS ON INDIA'S POTENTIAL DIRECTIONS

"I dream of an India that is strong, prosperous and inclusive, where each and every Indian can realize their hopes and aspirations."

— Narendra Modi

Reflective thoughts on the potential directions India might take following the path laid out by Modi's policies, offering a contemplative close to the narrative and inviting readers to engage with the evolving story of India.

Introduction

Under the stewardship of Narendra Modi, India has embarked on a transformative journey marked by ambitious reforms, strategic global positioning, and a vision to harness the country's potential to its fullest.

Modi's tenure has been characterized by a strong push towards economic development, digital innovation, social change, and a proactive role in international diplomacy. These efforts have been driven by a vision to position India as a global power, buoyed by its rich cultural heritage and a rapidly modernizing economy.

Modi's vision for India is deeply rooted in the belief that the nation's destiny is tied to its ability to adapt, innovate, and lead in an increasingly interconnected world. This vision has not only shaped the country's domestic policies and priorities but has also redefined its global stance. From the economic reforms aimed at boosting growth and attracting foreign investment to the Digital India campaign designed to bridge the digital divide, Modi's policies have sought to lay the groundwork for a more prosperous, inclusive, and forward-looking India.

Economic Growth and Innovation

The era of Narendra Modi's leadership has been particularly notable for its emphasis on economic growth and innovation.

By implementing a series of bold economic reforms, the government aimed to streamline the business environment, enhance fiscal discipline, and foster a spirit of entrepreneurship. Initiatives such as the Goods and Services Tax (GST) sought to unify the country into a single market, reducing tax complexity and encouraging trade. Moreover, the 'Make in India' campaign represented a significant push towards manufacturing and industrial development, aiming to position India as a global manufacturing hub.

Technological advancement and the digital economy have been central to Modi's vision of a new India. The Digital India initiative, with its focus on expanding internet access, improving digital literacy, and promoting digital services, has been pivotal in transforming the way services are delivered to the masses. This leap towards digitalization has not only spurred innovation but also created a fertile ground for startups, making India one of the fastest-growing startup ecosystems globally.

Despite these successes, the journey has not been without its challenges. Economic reforms, while transformative, have also been met with criticism and resistance.

The demonetization of high-value currency notes in 2016, intended to curb black money and encourage digital transactions, resulted in short-term economic disruption. Similarly, the implementation of GST, though beneficial in the long run, faced initial hurdles in adoption and compliance. Balancing the push for rapid economic growth with the need for sustainable and inclusive development remains an ongoing challenge.

Social and Cultural Evolution

India's social and cultural landscape has also witnessed significant changes under Modi's leadership.

Efforts to improve inclusivity, education, and healthcare have been at the forefront of social reforms. Schemes like the Swachh Bharat Abhiyan (Clean India Mission) not only aimed to improve sanitation and public health but also sought to instill a sense of civic responsibility towards cleanliness. The Ayushman Bharat program, the world's largest health insurance scheme, was launched to provide accessible healthcare to the underprivileged.

Cultural revitalization and the promotion of national identity have been other critical areas of focus. Modi's government has endeavored to celebrate India's cultural diversity while also reigniting interest in the country's heritage and traditional practices. However, these efforts have sparked debates over national identity and secularism, with critics arguing that the push for a singular cultural narrative may overlook the country's pluralistic essence.

Environmental and Global Stance

On the environmental front, India has made strides in integrating sustainability into its development agenda. Initiatives like the International Solar Alliance underscore Modi's vision of India playing a leading role in global environmental governance, particularly in the transition to renewable energy.

The commitment to significant reductions in carbon emissions and the promotion of sustainable practices reflect an acknowledgment of the pressing need to balance economic growth with environmental stewardship.

India's evolving role on the global stage under Modi has been marked by a more assertive foreign policy and strategic international partnerships. Modi's diplomacy has sought to elevate India's standing as a regional leader and a significant player in global affairs, navigating complex relationships with neighbors and major powers alike.

Potential Economic Trajectories

Looking towards the future, India's economic trajectory under the groundwork laid by Modi's policies is poised for diverse possibilities.

The nation's focus on digital innovation, coupled with its demographic dividend, positions it uniquely to leapfrog into new forms of economic activities, particularly in the digital and service sectors. Emerging technologies like artificial intelligence, blockchain, and the Internet of Things (IoT) could further propel India's economy, making it a global hub for technology and innovation. However, realizing this potential will require sustained efforts in education, skill development, and infrastructure investment to ensure that the workforce is equipped for the jobs of tomorrow.

The global economic landscape, characterized by shifting trade dynamics, rising protectionism, and the challenges of climate change, will also shape India's economic direction. Adapting to these changes while capitalizing on opportunities, such as the global supply chain realignment, could determine the pace and nature of India's economic growth. Furthermore, policies that encourage sustainable development and inclusive growth will be critical in addressing internal disparities and ensuring that the benefits of economic progress are broadly shared across the population.

Societal Trends and Cultural Identity

The societal and cultural landscape of India is likely to evolve under the influences of technological advancement, changing demographics, and global cultural flows. The increasing penetration of digital technology in rural and urban areas alike is transforming traditional lifestyles, education, and social interactions. This digital revolution could further democratize access to information, empower citizens, and foster a more informed and engaged society. As India continues to urbanize at a rapid pace, the challenges and opportunities of urban living will significantly impact societal trends. Issues such as housing, transportation, and sustainable urban development will require innovative solutions that balance growth with quality of life. Moreover, the country's demographic profile, with a large youth population, will drive demands for education, employment, and entertainment, potentially leading to shifts in cultural norms and values. India's cultural identity, enriched by its diversity, is likely to continue evolving as it interacts with global cultures. This interplay between the traditional and the modern, the local and the global, will shape the narrative of India's cultural evolution, potentially fostering a more inclusive and pluralistic society.

India's Global Role

Contemplating India's future global role, it is anticipated that the nation will assert stronger leadership in areas such as climate change, technology, and regional security. Modi's tenure has set the stage for India to leverage its growing economic and strategic capabilities to influence global governance and contribute to global peace and stability. As a leading voice for the Global South, India's advocacy for equity in international relations, including reforms in global institutions, will be crucial. The challenges of climate change present both a responsibility and an opportunity for India to lead by example through the adoption of green technologies and sustainable practices. In technology, India's burgeoning digital economy and expertise in information technology position it as a key player in shaping the global digital landscape.

Addressing Unresolved Issues

Despite the significant strides made under Modi's leadership, several critical challenges remain that will require attention and action in the years ahead. Economic disparities, environmental sustainability, and social cohesion stand out as areas needing focused efforts. Addressing the gap between India's urban and rural development, ensuring equitable access to resources and opportunities, and managing the environmental impact of rapid growth is paramount for sustainable progress. The importance of resilience and adaptability cannot be overstated in navigating these challenges. India's ability to adapt to technological, environmental, and economic shifts while ensuring inclusive growth will be crucial. The path forward involves not only leveraging India's strengths but also acknowledging and addressing its vulnerabilities with foresight and innovation.

The Role of Citizens

In shaping India's future, the role of its citizens is indispensable. Active engagement in democratic processes, from voting to civic participation, is crucial for the health and vitality of the republic. Furthermore, the spirit of entrepreneurship, community service, and social responsibility among the citizenry can drive grassroots change and complement governmental efforts in education, healthcare, and environmental stewardship. Encouraging a culture of dialogue and inclusivity is essential in addressing the complex challenges of a diverse society. Citizens' participation in constructive discourse, respecting differing viewpoints, and fostering a culture of tolerance and understanding can contribute significantly to social harmony and progress.

Concluding Reflections

Reflecting on Modi's tenure, the legacy of his leadership is marked by ambitious endeavors to transform India's economic landscape, social fabric, and global standing.

The initiatives and reforms undertaken during his leadership have set in motion changes that could shape India's trajectory for years to come. As India stands at the cusp of potential global leadership, the foundation laid in these years emphasizes innovation, inclusivity, and a proactive global stance.

Inspiring future generations, Modi's India presents a narrative of growth, challenges, and the relentless pursuit of greatness. It is a testament to the power of visionary leadership and collective action in steering a nation towards its aspirations. As India continues to navigate its path, the legacy of this era will be remembered for its contributions to shaping a prosperous, inclusive, and forward-looking nation.

Call to Action

This epilogue, while reflecting on the past and contemplating the future, is a call to action for every reader. It encourages continued engagement with the story of India's progress to contribute voices and efforts toward realizing the vision of a thriving, inclusive, and innovative nation. The journey of Modi's India is not just a story of a leader and his policies but a narrative of a nation and its people embracing change, facing challenges, and aspiring for a brighter future together.

ABOUT THE AUTHOR

Amit Prakash Sharma stands out as a beacon of intellectual and literary excellence, his profound insights cutting across many disciplines. Holding an MBA in Human Resource Management alongside a Diploma in Computer Application, Amit's scholastic achievements are further bolstered by a rich foundation in the arts and sciences, evident from his Bachelor's degrees in Hindi, English, Psychology, Political Science, and History from the esteemed Jiwaji University. This eclectic educational background underscores Amit's profound scholarly depth and ability to navigate and synthesize complex, interdisciplinary landscapes easily.

Currently enriching minds at the Indian Institute of Management Indore, Amit's contributions to academia are as vast as significant. Yet, his professional journey extends far beyond the academic realm. Amit has demonstrated remarkable versatility across various administrative roles, seamlessly blending managerial prowess with an in-depth appreciation for the arts and social sciences. This blend of skills has enabled him to navigate and contribute to diverse professional environments effectively. In the literary world, Amit Prakash Sharma has left an indelible mark. His roles as an author, editor, and publishing consultant have brought to life over 100 books, a testament to his eminent stature in the literary field.

His recognition as a top-rated professional on Upwork further highlights his prominence and high regard for his literary contributions.

Amit's intellectual curiosity is boundless. His explorations into psychology, philosophy, spirituality, and the arts have broadened his perspectives and significantly enriched his writing. His published works, including "Tathastu (So Be It! Amen!): A Soul's Promise," "The Enchanted Orchard of Mira and Milo," and "Eternal Souls, Separate Paths: Echoes of Love Across Time," reflect his narrative prowess. These works transcend mere storytelling; they are profound explorations into the intricacies of life, offering readers pathways to introspection, inspiration, and spiritual enlightenment.

Amit Prakash Sharma's writings represent a confluence of thought-provoking ideas and emotionally charged storytelling, transforming his books into experiences that resonate with readers long after turning the last page. His voice guides those navigating the complexities of the human condition, offering both enlightenment and a deeper connection to the world around them.

Through "Modi's India: Vision, Transformation, & the Road Ahead," Amit comprehensively explores India's socio-political evolution under Prime Minister Narendra Modi's leadership. Drawing on his vast academic knowledge and personal insights, Amit aims to present a balanced narrative that captures the essence of India's transformation, encouraging readers to engage with the content critically and constructively.

Amit Prakash Sharma's unique blend of scholarly acumen and narrative skill makes this book not just a scholarly analysis but a compelling story of a nation in flux. Readers are invited to join him in this nuanced exploration, a testament to the power of informed dialogue and the importance of understanding the multifaceted nature of governance and development in contemporary India.

CALL TO ACTION

ENGAGING WITH INDIA'S FUTURE

"The strength of a nation is determined by the joined hands of its people."

— Narendra Modi

This encourages readers to engage with the evolving narrative of India, fosters a dialogue around its future, and invites them to be part of the ongoing discourse surrounding Modi's impact on the nation.

Introduction

The "Call to Action" section begins by recapping India's transformative journey under Prime Minister Narendra Modi's leadership. It highlights the significant milestones achieved in terms of economic growth, digital innovation, and global diplomacy. For instance, the launch of the Digital India campaign in 2015 aimed to ensure government services are made available to citizens electronically by improving online infrastructure and increasing Internet connectivity. The Swachh Bharat Mission was initiated to eliminate open defecation and improve solid waste management.

"Digital India has become a way of life, particularly for the poor, marginalized, and for those in government."

— Narendra Modi.

This recap sets the stage for the ensuing discussion on the critical role of engagement in shaping the future of the nation. It underscores the book's aim to not only inform but also to inspire action and dialogue, thereby serving as a catalyst for readers to reflect on their role within the broader narrative of India's transformation.

Personal Reflection

The "Personal Reflection" section encourages readers to delve into introspection, considering how the transformations detailed in the book mirror their own experiences, beliefs, and aspirations for India. This segment introduces the stories of individuals and communities who have directly benefited from or been challenged by Modi's government's policies and initiatives.

For example, the Ujjwala Yojana scheme, launched in 2016, aimed to safeguard the health of women and children by providing them with a clean cooking fuel - LPG, thus avoiding the health hazards associated with cooking based on fossil fuels. By March 2019, the scheme had distributed over 70 million LPG connections to women below the poverty line.

"Clean cooking fuels are not just a recipe for better health; they are a precondition for empowerment and development."

— Dr. Harsh Vardhan, Indian Scientist and Politician

This narrative is complemented by personal testimonies from beneficiaries who experienced significant improvements in their health and daily lives, illustrating the tangible impact of such policies.

Another case study involves the Startup India initiative, which was unveiled to foster innovation and encourage entrepreneurship within the country. The story of a young entrepreneur from a small town who leveraged this initiative to start a tech company that now serves both national and international clients exemplifies the transformative potential of government support in empowering the youth and stimulating economic growth.

Community Dialogue

In advocating for discussions within communities, both online and offline, the book provides examples of how open dialogues can lead to broader understanding, challenge assumptions, and foster a culture of informed debate and tolerance. An illustrative example is the "Swachh Bharat Abhiyan" (Clean India Mission), where community-led initiatives significantly contributed to the mission's success in various locales. The narrative highlights how villages and cities organized cleanliness drives, awareness campaigns, and workshops on waste management, leading to substantial improvements in sanitation and public health.

"Sanitation and cleanliness are among the humblest of the civic virtues, and it is easy to underestimate their significance."

— Nelson Mandela.

The book also touches on the role of digital platforms in facilitating community dialogue. It mentions how social media has been used effectively to galvanize community action, share success stories, and encourage participation in government schemes. The story of a village that became open defecation-free (ODF) through the collective efforts of its residents, driven by a campaign on social media, serves as a testament to the power of community engagement and digital advocacy.

Civic Engagement

Moving on to "Civic Engagement," this section delves into the importance of active participation in India's democratic processes. It provides an analysis of voting trends, highlighting the increased voter turnout in recent elections as a sign of a more engaged electorate. The narrative emphasizes the significance of every vote, illustrating how close electoral contests have been swayed by a handful of votes, thereby underscoring the power of individual participation in shaping the nation's future.

"The ignorance of one voter in a democracy impairs the security of all."

— John F. Kennedy

Furthermore, the book discusses the role of citizens in local governance through mechanisms such as the "Jan Sunwai" (Public Hearing) and "Gram Sabhas" (Village Assemblies), where people can voice their concerns, suggest improvements, and directly engage with policymakers. The success story of a village that used its Gram Sabha to lobby for and eventually secure funding for a much-needed irrigation project exemplifies how civic engagement can lead to tangible outcomes and improve the quality of life for communities. Through these detailed narratives and data-driven analysis, the "Call to Action" section effectively underscores the myriad ways in which individuals can contribute to the ongoing narrative of India's development, fostering a proactive and participatory approach to the challenges and opportunities that lie ahead.

Social Initiatives

The segment on "Social Initiatives" shines a light on the power of individual and collective action in addressing societal challenges. It inspires readers with stories of individuals and groups who have made significant impacts in areas such as education, healthcare, environmental sustainability, and social justice.

A notable example is the story of a grassroots organization that launched a literacy program in rural areas, significantly reducing illiteracy rates and empowering communities with the knowledge and skills needed for self-sufficiency. This initiative not only facilitated access to education for children and adults alike but also sparked a movement towards educational reform in surrounding regions.

"Literacy is a bridge from misery to hope."

— Kofi Annan

In the healthcare sector, the narrative highlights a volunteer-driven campaign that successfully brought affordable medical care to remote villages. By setting up mobile clinics and leveraging telemedicine, the campaign addressed the acute shortage of healthcare services in underserved areas, dramatically improving health outcomes. The book also celebrates environmental efforts, such as a community-led reforestation project that revitalized a degraded forest area. This initiative not only restored biodiversity but also enhanced the local climate and provided sustainable livelihoods for the community, serving as a model for environmental conservation and economic development.

Continuous Learning

"Continuous Learning" emphasizes the importance of staying informed about India's political, economic, and social issues as a foundation for meaningful engagement and decision-making. It argues that an informed citizenry is crucial for the health of a democracy and the efficacy of governance. The section encourages readers to engage with a diverse range of sources for news and information, from traditional media to academic journals and beyond.

"An investment in knowledge pays the best interest."

— Benjamin Franklin

It suggests participating in public lectures, seminars, and workshops as ways to deepen understanding of complex issues and to stay abreast of the latest developments in various fields. Moreover, the narrative underscores the value of critical thinking and open-mindedness, urging readers to question and analyze the information they receive. By fostering a culture of continuous learning and intellectual curiosity, individuals can better contribute to informed public discourse and policymaking processes.

"Learning is not attained by chance; it must be sought for with ardor and attended to with diligence."

— Abigail Adams

Digital Engagement

In discussing "Digital Engagement," the book highlights the transformative potential of social media and digital platforms in advocating for change, raising awareness, and mobilizing support for various causes. Through case studies, it illustrates how digital campaigns have successfully influenced public opinion and policy decisions. One example is a viral social media campaign that brought attention to the plight of farmers in drought-stricken areas, leading to increased donations and government action to address water scarcity.

"Social media are a catalyst for the advancement of everyone's rights. It's where we're all getting our education."

— Ai Weiwei

Another case study features an online petition that garnered thousands of signatures, prompting legislative review and amendment of an outdated law affecting women's rights. The section also advocates for supporting digital literacy as a means to ensure wider participation in the digital dialogue about India's future.

It highlights successful programs that have equipped marginalized communities with digital skills, enabling them to access information, services, and opportunities in the digital age. By showcasing these examples, the "Call to Action" section conveys a powerful message: every individual has the potential to contribute to India's ongoing transformation. It concludes with a direct invitation for readers to take action in whatever capacity they can, reinforcing the idea that the journey towards a better future is a collective endeavor that requires the active participation of all stakeholders.

International Collaboration

The "International Collaboration" section underscores the significance of engaging with global perspectives and forming international partnerships to address the multifaceted challenges facing India and the world. This segment illustrates how cross-border collaborations have led to innovative solutions in areas such as technology, climate change, and public health. A prime example is India's participation in international environmental initiatives, contributing to and benefiting from global efforts to combat climate change. The book highlights India's role in the International Solar Alliance (ISA), a treaty-based intergovernmental organization that aims to mobilize more than $1 trillion in investments needed by 2030 for the massive deployment of solar energy. This not only positions India as a leader in renewable energy but also demonstrates the power of international cooperation in tackling global environmental challenges.

"Alone, we can do so little; together, we can do so much."

— Helen Keller

Another example detailed is the collaboration between Indian and foreign universities to advance research and development in various fields, leading to breakthroughs in medicine, engineering, and information technology.

These partnerships have not only enriched India's academic and scientific landscape but also facilitated cultural exchange and mutual understanding between nations.

Diaspora Engagement

"Diaspora Engagement" explores the critical role of the Indian diaspora in the country's development, leveraging their global experiences, skills, and networks. The narrative showcases stories of Non-Resident Indians (NRIs) and Persons of Indian Origin (PIOs) who have made significant contributions to India's socio-economic progress through investments, philanthropy, and knowledge exchange.

"The Indian diaspora has an incredible ability to contribute to the global community as well as to the development of India. They are a valuable bridge between India and the world."

— Narendra Modi

One highlighted story is of an NRI entrepreneur who established a technology incubator in India, providing mentorship and resources to start-ups and fostering innovation within the country. Another account details the efforts of a PIO-led charity that has funded numerous health and education projects in India, improving lives and communities. The section emphasizes the potential of the diaspora to act as bridges between India and the world, advocating for India's interests abroad and facilitating international partnerships. It calls on members of the diaspora to engage more deeply with India's developmental journey, whether through direct investment, participation in policy dialogue, or sharing their global perspectives and experiences.

A Collective Journey

The concluding section, "A Collective Journey," emphasizes that the future of Modi's India is not the responsibility of any single individual, government, or entity but a collective journey that involves every citizen.

It reinforces the idea that active participation, informed engagement, and a commitment to the common good are essential for navigating the challenges and seizing the opportunities that lie ahead. This final call to action invites readers to reflect on their role in this collective journey and to take practical steps towards contributing to India's future. Whether through civic engagement, supporting social initiatives, pursuing continuous learning, engaging digitally, fostering international collaboration, or contributing as part of the diaspora, every effort counts.

The narrative leaves readers feeling empowered, responsible, and motivated to act, bridging the gap between the insights offered in the book and the actionable steps they can take. It fosters a proactive and participatory approach, urging readers to be part of the ongoing narrative of India's development and to contribute to the shaping of a vibrant, inclusive, and prosperous future for the nation.

This detailed exploration of the "Call to Action" section in "Modi's India: Vision, Transformation, & the Road Ahead" not only concludes the narrative but also serves as a pivotal point for mobilizing readers to become active participants in India's ongoing transformation. By integrating real-life examples, case studies, expert insights, and data-driven analysis, this chapter aims to inspire, engage, and challenge readers to reflect on their contributions to the broader narrative of India's future.

"Every step you take is a step towards progress. No individual or organization can thrive in isolation. Our futures are intertwined."

— Ratan Tata.

The "Call to Action" section I crafted for the book "Modi's India: Vision, Transformation, & the Road Ahead" is a hypothetical construct designed to provide a comprehensive and engaging conclusion to a narrative about India's transformation under Prime Minister Narendra Modi's leadership.

The examples of individuals, policies, and initiatives mentioned in the section, such as the Ujjwala Yojana scheme, the Startup India initiative, and the International Solar Alliance, are real and have been part of Modi's administration's efforts to drive social, economic, and environmental progress in India.

However, the specific personal stories, community dialogues, and outcomes described within the "Personal Reflection," "Community Dialogue," "Civic Engagement," and other subsections are illustrative and intended to demonstrate how citizens might engage with and contribute to India's ongoing development. These examples aim to embody the principles of engagement, participation, and action encouraged in the section rather than to recount specific, verifiable instances of individual or community action.

The purpose of this detailed chapter is to inspire readers to reflect on their role in India's transformation, encouraging a sense of responsibility and proactive participation in shaping the country's future. It leverages the themes of vision, transformation, and the road ahead, central to Modi's tenure, to mobilize readers toward active involvement in India's development narrative.

Concluding Remarks

As the journey through "Modi's India: Vision, Transformation, & the Road Ahead" concludes, remember that exploration and dialogue do not end here. Your engagement and perspective are pivotal in continuing the conversation this book seeks to inspire. Here's how you can stay actively involved and contribute to this ongoing dialogue:

Join the Conversation Online: Share your thoughts, insights, and takeaways on social media using *#ModisIndiaBook* and *#ModisIndia*. Engage with fellow readers and contribute to discussions, helping to expand this crucial discourse to a wider audience.

Your voice is essential in fostering a community interested in the future of India's governance and development.

Participate in Community Dialogues: We encourage you to bring these conversations into your communities. Whether it's through organizing or participating in local discussions, book clubs, or forums, these platforms offer unique opportunities to delve deeper into the themes presented in the book and explore diverse viewpoints.

Follow Our Blog and Newsletter: Keep up to date with ongoing analyses, articles, and discussions related to the book's themes by subscribing to our blog and newsletter. Visit *https://www.scopage.com/blog* to subscribe and ensure you never miss an update.

Write a Review: If this book has enlightened, challenged, or inspired you, please consider sharing your experience by leaving a review on Amazon. Your feedback supports the author and helps guide potential readers.

Link: *https://www.amazon.com/author/amitprakashsharma*

Recommend to Friends and Family: If you found value in the insights provided, sharing the book with friends, family, and colleagues can amplify its impact. Spreading knowledge is a powerful catalyst for change.

Engage in Continuous Learning: Let this book serve as a starting point for exploring Indian politics and global leadership. Continue to read, research, and educate yourself on these dynamic subjects. Your involvement can ignite significant change and contribute to a more informed and engaged society. Together, let's continue building this conversation for a deeper understanding of Modi's India and the broader context of leadership and development in the modern world.

Connect with Us: Follow us on social media using *#ModisIndiaBook* and *#ModisIndia,* and join our community. Together, we can shape a more informed and engaged discourse on India's path forward.